P9-BZY-635

Cube Monkeys

Cube Monkeys

A Handbook for Surviving the Office Jungle

Editors of CareerBuilder.com

Second City Communications

Collins

An Imprint of HarperCollinsPublishers

CUBE MONKEYS. Copyright © 2007 by CareerBuilder.com. All rights reserved. Printed in the United States of America. No part of this book may be used or reproduced in any manner whatsoever without written permission except in the case of brief quotations embodied in critical articles and reviews. For information, address HarperCollins Publishers, 10 East 53rd Street, New York, NY 10022.

HarperCollins books may be purchased for educational, business, or sales promotional use. For information, please write: Special Markets Department, HarperCollins Publishers, 10 East 53rd Street, New York, NY 10022.

FIRST EDITION

Designed by Timothy Shaner, nightanddaydesign.biz

Library of Congress Cataloging-in-Publication Data

Cube monkeys : a handbook for surviving the office jungle / the editors of CareerBuilder.com, Second City Communications.
    p. cm.
  ISBN 978-0-06-135040-5
  1. Work—Humor. 2. Offices—Humor. I. Second City
Communications. II. Title.

  PN6231.W644C83 2007
  818'.602—dc22   2007023624

    07 08 09 10 11 ❖/RRD 10 9 8 7 6 5 4 3 2 1

Contents

1   Starting Your Morning Without Strangling Anyone 1

2   Combating Claustrophobia in Cubicle Land 15

3   Managing the Monkey in the Next Cube. 23

4   Bossology 41

5   Excuses for Everything 69

6   Meeting Schmetiquette 81

7   Small Talk 91

8   In Case of Emergency. 105

9   Break Time. 117

10   Happy Hour and Other Celebrations 129

11   I'm Outta Here! 141

    About the Authors 153

Chapter 1

Starting Your Morning
Without Strangling Anyone

Calling In Sick

Not ready to face another workday? Want to call in sick, but you've used the ol' Elmer-Fudd-voice-and-fake-sniffle combo a few too many times? For your own Ferris Bueller's Day Off, try one of these gems and start your workweek off right: catching up on soaps and Court TV shows while laughing sinisterly at how you outwitted "the man" once again.

- "It's a stomach thing. I think I ate some bad chicken. Or else it was the wine. Or the beer. Or the scotch. Or the ouzo. Or the cough syrup. But I think it was the chicken."
- "I think I have a bug in my system. I mean, a real bug. You see, I yawned when I rode my motorcycle over the weekend . . ."
- "I have disco fever. I just can't stop dancing."
- "I can't stop the ringing in my ears, so I can't hear what you're saying. If it's okay I take today off, just let me know. Wait, I can't hear you. I know, if it's okay I take a sick day, just don't say anything. Did you say anything? I'm just going to hang up. Is that okay? If it's . . ."
- "I have a cold . . . beer in my hand. Psych!"
- "I caught a computer virus. Did I ever mention I was bionic?"
- "I've got one of those twenty-four-hour things. What's it called . . . ? Oh yeah, a day off."
- "I'm being treated for attention deficit disorder. So I won't be able to—look, a bird! I *like* chocolate. Oh, my show is on. Bye!"
- "I took an overdose of placebos and I feel . . . Well, I don't know how I'm feeling."
- "I broke my leg. But I think it will be okay by tomorrow."

What to Wear

Another day in the office means another eight hours of observing soul-numbing regulations to fit into the corporate mold. The only chance you have at self-expression (besides that rad Jay-Z sticker on your cell phone—you are so street!) is the clothes you choose to wear. Your clothes give insight into who you are and give you a distinct advantage over those who show up to work naked. They say: "I am unique! I am a freethinking individual! And I can conform to a dress code!" Here's what the following outfits say about their owners.

MAN'S WARDROBE

COMPANY GOLF SHIRT AND KHAKIS. The "uniform." Years of middle management have slowly chipped every trace of individuality off your soul. Wearing anything else at this point might get you labeled as a "loose cannon."

$2,000 ARMANI SUIT. You have arrived and have more tact than to wear a sandwich board reading, "I'm rich, suckahs!" It doesn't matter the cut or the color—it's Armani! And yes, your hair plugs look ridiculous, but nobody is going to say anything because you can have them fired—or maybe even killed! The suit is that good.

OLD IRON MAIDEN T-SHIRT. Yeah, you may work in the mail room, but at least you still know how to party!

THE SWEATER VEST. Why not? Maybe getting beat up at work is more rewarding than getting beat up at school.

CORPORATE CLUB WEAR. That black-on-blacker-black silk shirt is not just clothing; it's hip and stylish fashion. Older folks assume the wearer is in touch with today's youth and emerging trends. Younger folks assume he deals drugs on the side. In any case, he'll get promoted before you will.

COWBOY BOOTS AND HAT. You're either an actual cowboy or a high-profile attorney.

POLYESTER TWO-PIECE BLUE SUIT WITH WRINKLED WHITE SHIRT AND BLUE-AND-RED-STRIPED TIE. Lonely, so very lonely.

WOMAN'S WARDROBE

BEIGE TWO-PIECE BUSINESS SUIT. Smart and highly practical, these suits can go from the office to the hamper back to the office because you didn't have time to go to the cleaners after Delvin got his head stuck in a bait bucket. They usually have rich textures and subtle patterns—perfect for camouflaging baby vomit.

$2,000 ARMANI SUIT. You have arrived and most likely in a Hummer that takes up three parking spots.

BOYFRIEND SWEATER. You have a boyfriend! Nya-nya nya-nya nya-nyaaa!

PINK CASHMERE TWO-PIECE TOP AND PEARLS. You're perky, punctual, and professional! You are sooo excited to be working here because your sorority sister works just three floors up and you have lunch together, like, every day! It's a scream!

RED TIGHT MIDTHIGH LEATHER SKIRT. "I'm finding me a husband!"

GREEN-AND-RED SWEATER WITH RED-NOSED REINDEER ON FRONT AND CANDY-CANE TRIM. You have holiday cheer with capital *H-C*! Your enthusiasm is infectious, especially this time of year. If the Secret Santa program is canceled this year because management insists on "only non-religiously-affiliated-holiday recognition" you will kill everybody in the office.

The Neck Noose
A (Mostly Fictional) History of the Necktie

Most companies don't require employees to wear a uniform. What you wear to the office is a personal choice, except, of course, for the necktie. So how did the neck noose, which seems to have no function other than increasing men's physical discomfort, become mandatory in the workplace? Let's take a look at the history of this bizarre fashion accessory.

210 BC Shih Huang-ti, China's first emperor, demands that all officers in the army wear matching neckties. It does little to improve morale, especially given that the Chinese military's severance package still involves being buried alive in the emperor's tomb.

113 AD The Roman emperor Trajan regularly wears a knotted necktie during battle, believing that it protects his neck from injury. As it turns out, his theory is very, very wrong.

1419 Henry V of England issues a proclamation that all countrymen must wear neckties to identify their social standing. He enjoys walking the streets of London and tugging on the commoners' ties, often saying something vaguely derogatory like, "I need that report on my desk by Friday." His comments are considered gibberish, as few fifteenth-century serfs have any idea what a "report" is.

The Neck Noose

1620 The necktie (or "cravate") is introduced to France by Croatian mercenaries and becomes an instant hit. The word "cravate" is roughly translated as "working in a confined space until you're forced into early retirement and given a gold watch."

1680 King Charles II becomes the first member of English royalty to embrace the necktie, and he collects a staggering array of styles and colors, including several made entirely of old meat. He expires during a public ceremony after consuming a poultry tie infected with salmonella.

1785 The German necktie, known as a "stock," becomes popular among the Berlin elite. Because of their name, stocks are often confused with "stockades," a device commonly used for punishing criminals. The error is eventually corrected, but as many Germans soon realize, there is very little difference between the two.

1845 Colorful neckties are introduced in Cambridge University, resulting in the misconception that paisley matches with anything.

1928 The clip-on tie is invented, allowing millions of businesspeople to announce to the world, "I do not have the intellectual faculties necessary to remember that the rabbit goes into the hole and around the tree."

1937 The Duke of Windsor invents an elaborate and overly complicated tying method known as

The Neck Noose

"the Windsor knot." When done correctly, it cuts off circulation to the brain, causing dizziness, fainting, vertigo, nosebleeds, and occasionally aneurysms. Windsor's innovation continues to be popular among self-hating office workers to this day.

1968 Neckties fall out of favor due to the predominance of hippies. Not coincidentally, the era also sees a rise in dancing naked in the mud.

1983 Neckties come back into vogue during the Reagan era, mostly by very confused businessmen who assume (wrongly, as it turns out) that it distracts coworkers from noticing their parachute pants.

1992 Grateful Dead lead singer Jerry Garcia introduces a line of neckties, replacing patchouli and ponytails as a convenient way to identify the office druggie.

1998 Neckties become "ironic" during the Internet boom, not because of their unconventional designs but because the office workers who wear them will be unemployed within a few months.

2007 Steve Jobs introduces the iTie, which not only complements a navy suit perfectly, but also acts as a PDA, cell phone, e-mail messenger, and digital music player. Unfortunately, the first owner spills soup on it and dies of electrocution.

Everybody into the Carpool: The Art of Getting to Work Without Spending a Dime

Not only do employers expect you to take forty-plus hours out of your week to sit in a cramped little cubicle, they expect you to get there yourself. Traffic takes forever, and with the price of gas skyrocketing, soon it'll cost you more to get to work than you're going to take home in your measly little paycheck. Well, not anymore. With these money-saving tips, you'll soon be able to supersize your lunch—and get change back to boot.

- Invite a coworker to dinner and drug him. When he comes to in the morning greet him with a cup of coffee and say, "You still look a little groggy. I'll drive us to work in your car!" Be sure to hide his wallet in your couch so you can get a ride home.

- You pay taxes, right? Hijack a bus.

- Start a carpool. When it finally comes your turn to drive, pick a fight with the other members of the carpool and quit in a huff. Repeat as necessary.

- Biking is a fun and practical way to get to work for free—if you're a total dork.

- Take the train to work. What's that, you say? Your city doesn't have a commuter rail system? No problem. Just hop a boxcar on a freight train and live the romantic life of a hobo. It'll be something to tell your grandkids about . . . if you don't get shived.

- Why not just crash at work? You can stash some clean clothes and microwave burritos in a desk drawer. At night you could sit in other people's cubicles and pretend you're them. Maybe then you'll feel loved.

Late for Work Again?
Fail-Proof Conversation Stoppers

So you overslept. Again. It's not the end of the world. But to hear your boss rant and rave you'd think your company was making cruise missiles instead of . . . whatever the hell they do. Here are some handy phrases that will stop the inquisition dead in its tracks.

66 Oh, it's *spring* forward, *fall* back. If only there were some mnemonic device to help you remember that. *99*

66 I saw that you weren't in the office, so I went out looking for you. *99*

66 I heard you once say, don't come in until you're prepared to work. And for me, that's about twelve, twelve-thirty. *99*

66 Time is an illusion, an artificial construct. This is the belief of my people. *99*

66 I was here at nine sharp and got right to work. But it turns out I was in the wrong cube. They do all really look alike, don't they? *99*

66 Late? Am I? Am I actually late for today? Or really early for tomorrow? *99*

Top Ten Suitable Greetings for When You'd Rather Say, "Leave Me Alone!"

TOP 10

Some things are better left unsaid, like entire conversations with annoying coworkers. You know the situation: you come in the office with your first cup of coffee in hand, wanting only to sit at your desk, fully wake up, and focus on the day's work. But before your butt hits the chair, the office chatterbox steps in front of you, ready to trap you into a twenty-minute

"Good Morning, I Hate You"

conversation about the fascinating television show he or she watched last night. Here are some useful phrases to nip the conversation in the bud. Keep in mind, sometimes offense is the best defense.

1. "Can't talk! Last night I converted to Buddhism and took a vow of—damn!"

2. "Give me just a second." Close your eyes and say softly to yourself, "It's okay to ask coworkers for money, it's okay to ask coworkers for money . . ."

3. "I'm too busy picturing you naked to talk to you right now."

4. "Can't . . . talk . . . coffee . . . poisoned . . . must . . . get . . . help."

5. "Can this wait? My fingernails are slowly growing right now and it's a little distracting."

6. "Next one who talks hates babies, starting now!"

7. "Good morning? Who the hell are you, the morning police?!"

8. "Punch me in the stomach! Go ahead; hit me right in the gut!" (When they do, roll on the ground moaning until they leave.)

9. "Do you have the blue sedan in the parking lot with the smashed front end? Well, I mean now it is."

10. "Don't talk, kiss me! Kiss me now!"

Are You a Morning Person, or Just an Ass?

Do you arrive at work with an extra spring in your step? Or are you more likely to take a swing at anyone who steps in front of you? Take this quiz and see how you rate on the surly scale.

1. When riding the elevator to your office each morning, you greet your fellow employees by . . .

❏ a. Giving each and every person a hug, and wishing them "another glorious day."

❏ b. Grunting while loudly slurping your coffee.

❏ c. Unleashing an endless string of expletives about having to stop at every floor.

2. A meeting is scheduled for 9 a.m. You . . .

❏ a. Arrive twenty minutes early, bringing a fresh batch of your mom's famous homemade egg quiche.

❏ b. Sit, zone out, review someone's notes after lunch.

❏ c. Show up to meeting wearing shades and listening to your iPod.

3. What do you typically accomplish before lunch?

❏ a. You've finished all your reports, replied to all your e-mails, and decorated the conference room with an array of colorful spring flowers.

❏ b. You've listened to your voice mail messages while playing twenty-seven consecutive games of computer solitaire.

❏ c. You've hissed menacingly at anyone who attempted to open the window shades within twenty yards of your cubicle.

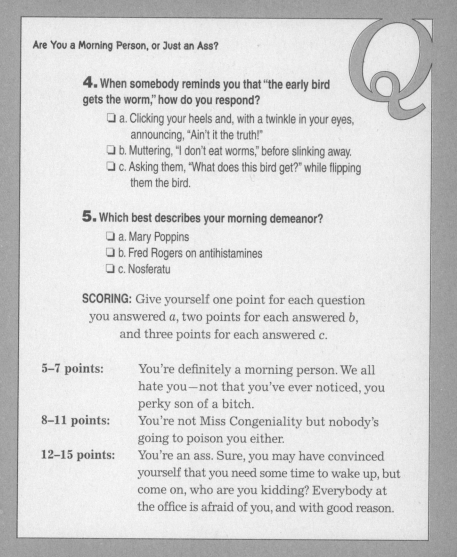

Are You a Morning Person, or Just an Ass?

4. When somebody reminds you that "the early bird gets the worm," how do you respond?

❑ a. Clicking your heels and, with a twinkle in your eyes, announcing, "Ain't it the truth!"
❑ b. Muttering, "I don't eat worms," before slinking away.
❑ c. Asking them, "What does this bird get?" while flipping them the bird.

5. Which best describes your morning demeanor?

❑ a. Mary Poppins
❑ b. Fred Rogers on antihistamines
❑ c. Nosferatu

SCORING: Give yourself one point for each question you answered *a*, two points for each answered *b*, and three points for each answered *c*.

5–7 points: You're definitely a morning person. We all hate you—not that you've ever noticed, you perky son of a bitch.

8–11 points: You're not Miss Congeniality but nobody's going to poison you either.

12–15 points: You're an ass. Sure, you may have convinced yourself that you need some time to wake up, but come on, who are you kidding? Everybody at the office is afraid of you, and with good reason.

Getting Your Morning Caffeine Fix
Without Resorting to the Office Sludge

Sure, the old coffeepot is great for gathering around to hear the latest office gossip, but the stuff that's in it? Forget it. Not only is the coffee your company buys made from the cheapest beans available, no one has cleaned the pot since . . . well, no one's ever cleaned the pot. And every once in a while, some wisenheimer slips in a pot of decaf. Here are some alternatives to the morning "grind."

Designer coffee. Unless you're going to put an überload of cream in it, this stuff is harsh. But its strength is perfect for that "slap you in the mouth" morning wake-up. . . or for stripping furniture. → **8 Jitters**

Energy drink. Best mixed with vodka. Of course, doing so cancels out the effects entirely, but at least it will make the day go by a lot faster. → **5 Jitters**

Fruit smoothie. It's got "fruit" in the name, so it must be healthy, right? Throw in some ginkgo extract and you won't be able to blink for days. → **4 Jitters**

Herbal tea. Give me a break. What are you, a hippie? → **1 Jitter**

Diet pills. Work like a charm for the morning after. And you can quit anytime you want. No really. . . you can. . . you can quit. . . anytime. → **10 Jitters**

"All natural" energy pills. It'll give you all the alertness of an illegal pill-popping junkie, but without the paranoia and imminent danger of serving prison time. → **3 Jitters**

Cola. A potent combination of sugar and caffeine that'll get you going. But when you crash from the sugar high, you'll need another. . . and another. . . and another. → **7 Jitters**

Prune juice. Puts the *B-M* in your "Big Morning." If that doesn't get you up, nothing will. → **2 Jitters**

Of course, if none of this works, you could always get plenty of rest, exercise, and eat a balanced diet. . . nawww!

13

Chapter 2
Combating Claustrophobia in Cubicle Land

Feng Shui Your Cube

Do you ever wonder why you're not the boss? Do you wonder why you're stressed out, overworked, and underappreciated? The answer is simple: the items on your desk are not arranged properly! Using the ancient art of feng shui to improve the flow of positive energy, or chi, will guarantee you will be rich, healthy, successful, and physically attractive in a matter of hours.*

- Mirrors are excellent for redirecting negative energy. They're also an excellent distraction from work, providing ample opportunities to stare at your own reflection and say, "Hey, good-looking, come here often?"

- An array of scented candles can enhance your sense of relaxation, especially if you run around the office and knock them over, like Sting in that Police video from the 1980s.

- To succeed in business, make sure your desk faces east. If your desk doesn't face east, demand that the office be remodeled. Keep demanding until you are fired.

- A fountain is excellent for serenity. If you don't have a fountain, start a small fire until the sprinklers come on.

- All Dilbert cartoons should face west.

- If you are finding your cube difficult to feng shui, try Wang Chung.

*This is not a guarantee.

Business Books to Impress the Big Dogs

Show the muckety-mucks you're a real go-getter by keeping up with the latest bestsellers on the stands. They can give invigorating perspective for the days ahead ... or serve as anchors for a cubicle fort made out of blankets.

How to Win Friends and Influence People and Then Use That to Destroy Them

NOW, DISCOVER YOUR STRENGTHS: LATER, GIVE IN TO YOUR WEAKNESSES

FINK AND GROW RICH: Snitching on Your Coworkers For Fun and Profit

WHAT COLOR ARE YOUR PARACHUTE PANTS? Time to Update Your Wardrobe

THE MILLIONAIRE NEXT DOOR: And If He's So Rich, Why Is He Living in Your Crappy Neighborhood?

WHO MOVED MY CHEESE? No, Seriously, It Was Right Here

GEEKONOMICS: How to Bribe the IT Guys So They'll Give You a New Laptop

THE TIPPLING POINT: Getting Your Coworkers Drunk to Get the Office Dirt

GOOD TO GRATE: Annoy Your Boss Until You Get That Promotion

THE ONE-SECOND MANAGER: When One Minute Is Just Too Damn Long

Cube Etiquette

Want to put your cube neighbor into a full nelson, but not sure if etiquette will allow? Ms. Cube-Manners, our resident advice columnist, answers a few of the most popular questions regarding proper cubicle etiquette and decorum.

Dear Ms. Cube-Manners,

My coworkers get annoyed whenever I pop my head over the partition of their cubicles to ask a question or borrow office supplies or listen in on their personal phone conversations. Are they just being too sensitive, or should I respect their privacy?

The Prairie Dog

Dear Prairie Dog,
Privacy in the workplace? Give me a break! It's the price we pay for the new "open office environment." If your coworkers don't like it, tell them they should consider applying for a position where you don't have to interact much with people, like a hermit or a monk or management.

Dear Ms. Cube-Manners,

The woman in the next cubicle is a good worker and I consider her a friend but she has an annoying habit. She constantly hums to herself during the day. I've tried ignoring it and wearing earplugs but I still hear her. It is very distracting and starting to affect my work. What should I do?

Hum-Bugged

Dear Hum-Bugged,

Perhaps you should show a little more sympathy toward your coworker. Most hummers lead a secret life of shame because they can't remember the words. In fact, legislation is now passing through Congress to have this affliction covered by insurance. Next time you hear your coworker humming, why not join in and hum as well, or perhaps accompany her with a musical instrument? But don't harmonize. That's just annoying.

Dear Ms. Cube-Manners,

I've personalized my cubicle with my collection of teddy bears from all fifty states. Recently, one of my coworkers said it looked unprofessional. But she has pictures of her family pinned all over her wall. Is it my fault I don't have family photos to put in my cubicle? Who's right?

Beary Confused

Dear Beary Confused,

Stop writing me, Mom.

19

Office Supplies: What to Use in a Pinch

On your first day of work, your HR representative probably showed you where the office supply closet is. But by your second day, you realized that knowing where the office supply closet is and getting your office supplied are two totally different things. The watchword of the modern office is "flexibility." Here are some creative ideas for improvising in a pinch.

PROBLEM: You've printed out all those saucy e-mails from your girlfriend, but you can't find a paper clip to hold them together.

SOLUTION: Just snatch a bobby pin from that uptight girl in Accounting. (And you'll be helping her, too!)

PROBLEM: You run out of staples just as you need to collate that thirty-page report on ways to reduce paper use in the office.

SOLUTION: Bandages from the office first-aid kit will hold those papers together and they're practically invisible—if you use flesh-toned paper.

PROBLEM: No rubber band, just when you need to bind together the stack of mix CDs you burned on your computer.

SOLUTION: Nab one from the braces of the new intern when she's yakking about her plans for the weekend.

PROBLEM: You're filling out a W-9 and you put down 111 dependents instead of one. You could really use some Wite-Out, but you can't find it anywhere.

SOLUTION: Use cardboard and scissors to create 111 "fictional" children. Care for them as your own.

PROBLEM: You need to glue some incriminating photos to that blackmail letter you're sending to your boss, but the glue stick in your desk dried out in 1994.

SOLUTION: Create a MySpace account for your boss and upload the photos instead. Include URL address in your blackmail letter.

PROBLEM: No thumbtack to post your "enemies list" on the office bulletin board.

SOLUTION: Use a fork from a local fast-food restaurant. Looks vaguely threatening but won't hold up in court.

PROBLEM: You're supposed to turn in your budget numbers but you don't have any blank CDs.

SOLUTION: Just turn in an old Led Zeppelin CD. By the time your boss figures it out, she'll be groovin' to the tunes.

Chapter 3

Managing the Monkey in the Next Cube

Your Most Annoying Coworkers: A Field Guide

Ever feel like you're on a safari at work? Maneuvering your way through treacherous terrain, dangerously close to a species that may want to eat you for lunch or, worse yet, eat with you? Grab your binoculars and the field guide below to identify telltale traits of your most annoying coworkers and to learn how to survive an encounter with them.

THE CHEESEBALL *(Swissus Discus)*

The guy who pretends his hand is a gun and shoots while winking at you. Variations include the high five, the low five, any other fives (stop with the fives!), as well as the fake punch to the stomach.

TIP: *Pretend that you're truly scared and wrestle his fake finger gun from his hand, pounding his wrist on the desk to make him drop it. Remember to report him to HR for bringing a deadly weapon to the office. It's the only way he'll learn.*

THE SOAP OPERA STAR *(Generalius Hospitalius)*

The coworker who has more drama in her life than *The Young and the Restless* and feels compelled to share all the intimate details about her boyfriend, cat, diet, cat, neighbors, cat, car, cat, family, cat, cat, cat, cat, cat, cat, cat, cat.

TIP: *Bet her she can't fit twenty marshmallows in her mouth.*

THE CATERER *(E Pluribus Foodum)*
Who knew you could roast a pig in a cube? This coworker brings in every kind of food and proceeds to set up a buffet in his area . . . making the office smell like a college cafeteria.

TIP: *Remember, a little Ex-Lax is the perfect garnish for any smorgasbord.*

THE CRUISE DIRECTOR *(Julius McCoylius)*
The coworker who feels she needs to celebrate something every day—birthdays, new office supplies, the anniversary of her first FedEx.

TIP: *Invent a religion that allows you to celebrate only your own holidays and inform your coworker that the daily celebrations bring up painful memories from your childhood when you weren't allowed to participate with others.*

Your Most Annoying Coworkers: A Field Guide

THE CRYBABY *(BooHookium)*

Does every conversation at work end in waterworks? Does the littlest thing set off Niagara Falls in the next cube?

> **TIP:** *If you can't beat 'em, join 'em. Everyone can use a good cry. Occasionally, ask him or her to hold you.*

THE CRITIC *(Buzzicous Killium)*

There's no pleasing this nitpicking connoisseur of complaints and quibbler extraordinaire.

> **TIP:** *Every time the critic starts bellyaching, stick your fingers in your ears and rock back and forth while saying, "The voices are back, the voices are back."*

THE MEGAPHONE *(Muzzleupacous)*

Do you feel as if you work in an airport or on the floor of the stock exchange? The Megaphone answers every call on speakerphone and doesn't care if it's personal or business.

> **TIP:** *Invite coworkers to pull up chairs around*

Your Most Annoying Coworkers: A Field Guide

*his or her desk, eagerly listening in while eating
popcorn. Make sure to take detailed notes on
personal calls for the employee newsletter.*

THE MIA *(Harrius Houdinius)*

This person spends more time on the golf course than
on the job and is never to be found anytime there's
real work to be done.

TIP: *Set up an electronic fence, so every time
the MIA goes out of boundaries, he or she gets
shocked.*

THE HYPOCHONDRIAC *(Sniffle-up-agous)*

Does a paper cut require an EMT? Does spilled
Coffee-mate in the break room provoke an immed-
iate call to the Centers for Disease Control?

TIP: *Send 'em over the edge by convincing
everyone in the office to wear a hazmat suit
and start screaming when the Hypochondriac
walks in without one.*

Are You the Office Party Animal?

Were you the kind of college student who drank to excess every night and could always be counted on to do something wild and outrageous? Most of us stopped partying till dawn when we entered the workplace, but some people—hint, hint—don't realize that having perpetually puffy and bloodshot eyes isn't quite as cute at thirty-six as it was at twenty-four. Take the following quiz to find out if you share any traits with the Office Party Animal.

1. Your cubicle . . .

❏ a. Is always neat and tidy.
❏ b. Has a certain homey charm.
❏ c. Has been moved to the strip club down the street.

2. You prepare for the annual office Christmas party . . .

❏ a. A few days in advance.
❏ b. A few weeks in advance.
❏ c. In June.

3. How do you take your coffee?

❏ a. With just a hint of cream.
❏ b. With a few packets of sugar.
❏ c. With gin.

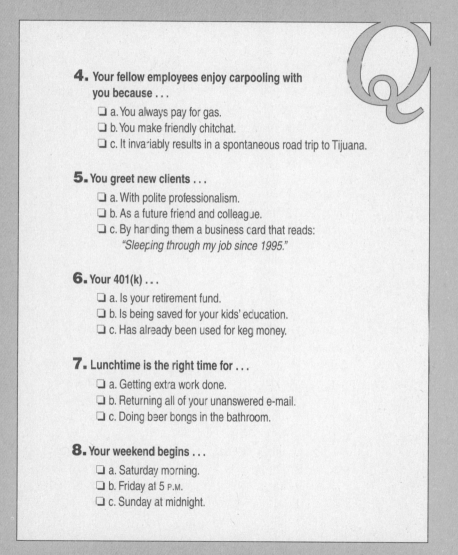

4. Your fellow employees enjoy carpooling with
you because . . .

   ❏ a. You always pay for gas.
   ❏ b. You make friendly chitchat.
   ❏ c. It invariably results in a spontaneous road trip to Tijuana.

5. You greet new clients . . .

   ❏ a. With polite professionalism.
   ❏ b. As a future friend and colleague.
   ❏ c. By handing them a business card that reads:
      "Sleeping through my job since 1995."

6. Your 401(k) . . .

   ❏ a. Is your retirement fund.
   ❏ b. Is being saved for your kids' education.
   ❏ c. Has already been used for keg money.

7. Lunchtime is the right time for . . .

   ❏ a. Getting extra work done.
   ❏ b. Returning all of your unanswered e-mail.
   ❏ c. Doing beer bongs in the bathroom.

8. Your weekend begins . . .

   ❏ a. Saturday morning.
   ❏ b. Friday at 5 P.M.
   ❏ c. Sunday at midnight.

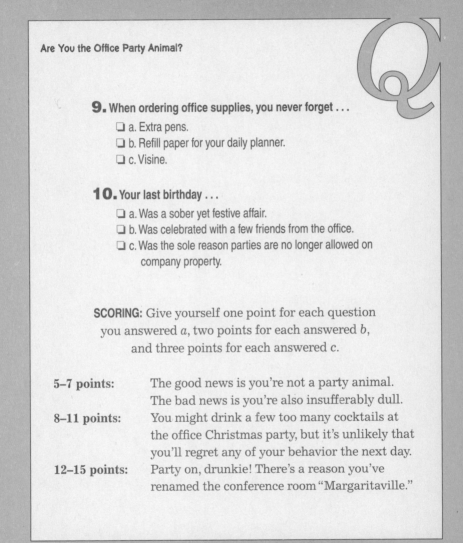

Are You the Office Party Animal?

9. When ordering office supplies, you never forget . . .
❏ a. Extra pens.
❏ b. Refill paper for your daily planner.
❏ c. Visine.

10. Your last birthday . . .
❏ a. Was a sober yet festive affair.
❏ b. Was celebrated with a few friends from the office.
❏ c. Was the sole reason parties are no longer allowed on company property.

SCORING: Give yourself one point for each question you answered *a*, two points for each answered *b*, and three points for each answered *c*.

5–7 points: The good news is you're not a party animal. The bad news is you're also insufferably dull.

8–11 points: You might drink a few too many cocktails at the office Christmas party, but it's unlikely that you'll regret any of your behavior the next day.

12–15 points: Party on, drunkie! There's a reason you've renamed the conference room "Margaritaville."

Things You Don't Want to Hear from the New Coworker

Working in a modern office often means working in close quarters. When a new employee joins the team, the anticipation can be agonizing. Will she be rude, lewd, or a real prude? Will he be sleepy, weepy, or downright creepy? Here are some red-flag phrases you don't want to hear from the new cube monkey.

66 Just out of curiosity: you're not one of those nosy troublemakers that watches *America's Most Wanted*, are you? 99

66 I've had this fever ever since I visited that poultry farm in China. Can I borrow your ChapStick?"

66 Things are slow. Let's Jazzercise! 99

66 Where do you live? Oh wait, never mind. Say, did you ever get that garage door fixed? 99

66 Don't worry, I don't keep it loaded. 99

66 Is it just me, or can you taste colors? Man, I think somebody laced the coffee. Oh wait, that was me! 99 *(Laughs hysterically.)*

66 I can tell already that we're gonna be BFFs. Hey, wanna have a sleepover tonight? 99

66 Don't open my drawer. I'm making cheese in there. 99

66 I'm in *Guinness World Records* for loudest gum chewer. 99

66 I'm the boss's niece. 99

Becoming the Office Gossip

The workplace is governed by two seemingly conflicting laws: (1) "Knowledge is power." (2) "A little knowledge can be a dangerous thing." The Office Gossip stands firmly in the intersection of these two laws, using as little knowledge as possible to anoint himself (or herself) with maximum power—and while he's at it, destroying his coworkers' reputations. If you want to become the most feared and influential person in your office, here are a few helpful tips to get you started:

- Use your Google skills to find an interesting bit about someone who may or may not be the "John Smith" in your office, then casually mention it in your next conversation.
- Master the art of popping up over the wall of cubicles suddenly.
- Drink upwards of twenty-two cups of coffee a day, just for an excuse to jaw around the pot.
- Don't wait for gossip to come to you. Spend your break rummaging through wastebaskets or piecing together scraps of paper from the office shredder.
- If confronted about a juicy story you've been spreading, suddenly "realize" that you were thinking of an old *Boston Legal* episode.
- To appear trustworthy, insist on hugging everybody who initiates a conversation.
- Always have a smug expression. This will let your coworkers know that you're armed with "a good one."
- Take three juicy parts from three different stories and change the names. This way, everything is kinda true and you gain credibility.
- Casual flirting between coworkers doesn't always mean that they're having an affair. Ignore this and spread salacious rumors anyway.
- When in doubt, just make something up.

The Uncomfortable Conversation: How to Tell a Coworker He Stinks

Every office has one: The Stink Bomb. The Human Whoopee Cushion. The Close Talker who always has something urgent to tell you right after eating a tuna melt. Below are a few ways to hint to your odoriferous coworker that he should scrub-a-dub-dub.

DO appeal to his funny bone: "Knock-knock. Who's there? No one, because you stink."

DON'T place a beautiful fragrant bouquet of flowers on the offender's desk with a card reading, "Have a nice day. You smell like feet."

DO challenge your coworker to a Febreze fight. When you're done, sniff and say, "That's better."

DON'T change her caller ID to "The Stinkster."

DO call him out in the next meeting by saying, "Johnson, you're a smelly bastard; what's your take on this?"

DON'T ask the offender to settle a bet: did she roll in a dead squirrel or a dead seagull on the way to work?

DO try a subtle approach like, "Hey, Bob, how do you think fifty Altoids would taste?"

DON'T overtly faint every time your coworker opens her mouth, especially when you're on the other side of the room.

DO hang a bunch of car freshener pine trees around his cube. When questioned, say, "It's to support the trees. You're not anti-tree, are you?"

DON'T draw those wavy cartoon lines above the photo on her employee ID.

DO yell a friendly, "Smell ya later!" at him when leaving work. Then, "No, really, I'll smell you later."

How to Improve Office Morale

In a perfect world, an office would function like a colony of ants; workers would move with emotionless precision, all working for the greater good of the corporation and eating the limbs of rival species. But we humans can be an emotional lot, and if one coworker is in a sour mood, it can spread in a domino effect until the whole department is adrift in a sea of suicidal despair and fluorescent lighting. So, it is important to keep morale high and people's minds off the meaningless routine that is their daily lives. Mark your calendar each month with reminders of ways to spread office cheer.

DAY 1

Organize a company layoff office pool. Anyone who correctly identifies soon-to-be terminated employees gets a coupon for a free appetizer at Applebee's.

DAY 5

High-Five Day! All office interaction must be accompanied by a high five. Those who refuse to participate should be scolded with "Don't leave me hanging."

DAY 7

Sit at desk weeping loudly so everyone else's mood seems better by contrast.

DAY 9

Use the ol' smash-the-BlackBerry-with-a-hammer gag.

DAY 12

Piñata Day! Put on a blindfold and walk around the office swinging a bat until someone brings one in.

DAY 15

Coffee Drink-Off. Find out who can consume the most caffeine before his or her liver implodes. The first one to require emergency transport to the hospital wins.

DAY 17

Take credit for other people's work in the weekly meeting. It promotes a strong team environment.

DAY 19

Everyone loves a good polka!

DAY 20

Casual Sex Friday!

DAY 25

Memory Lane Day! Remind office of all the benefits that have been cut over the last ten years.

DAY 27

Draw horns and mustaches on pictures of coworkers' spouses — guaranteed laugh!

DAY 30

Field trip to Build-a-Beer!

Top Ten Ways to End a Conversation with a Talkative Coworker

TOP 10

Over the last five years the need to talk to coworkers has been virtually eliminated by the use of e-mail and instant messaging. However, from time to time you may still find yourself giving up valuable "face time" to people who drone on and on about their kids, their pets, what they dreamed last night, or ways to solve clients' problems—it's all pretty much the same. Getting stuck in one of these one-sided conversations takes up precious time that could be used slacking off in a myriad of other ways. You owe it to the company and yourself to shut such people up. Here are some tips:

"Shut Your Piehole!"

1. When you've grown weary of the conversation, look confused and say, "I'm sorry, I don't speak Italian." Your coworker will try to insist he isn't speaking Italian. Just keep saying, "I'm sorry, that's Italian; I don't speak Italian." This one is all about commitment!

2. Try throwing peanuts into her mouth as she talks.

3. At the slightest indication of humor, begin laughing hysterically. Continue laughing nonstop until quitting time.

4. Reach into your pocket and grab your cell phone as if it is vibrating. Throw it at him and run.

5. During her ramblings, pretend to become offended. Say, "I've had just about enough of your thinly veiled come-ons!" Then, storm off in a huff.

6. After enduring a lengthy story from the offender, bill him for your time.

7. Cutting people off is rude, but cutting yourself off isn't. At some point in the dreadful conversation say, "You know what I think of all this . . ." Then walk quickly away.

8. Keep several ketchup packets hidden under your shirt. When the conversation gets to be too much to bear, smack your hand against your chest, breaking open the packets. Drop to the ground and yell, "Sniper!"

9. Tattoo the words "shut" and "up" on your eyelids; drift off to sleep.

10. Air horn to the face.

How to Get Your Coworker Fired: A Step-by-Step Plan

That person in the next cubicle may seem friendly enough, but he is your sworn enemy. As long as he is around and being productive, you may never get that fat promotion you've been dreaming about. Follow this three-week plan, and you'll be able to get rid of the competition once and for all.

Week One: Setting the Stage

The key to getting an employee fired is encouraging bad behavior that makes him look not only unprofessional but potentially litigious. Start slow, as you don't want your mark to wise up and start dismissing your admittedly unhelpful advice.

MONDAY: If the bathroom is occupied, remind him that the employee kitchen has a sink, and "a drain is a drain."

WEDNESDAY: Act surprised that he, unlike every other employee who has ever worked for the company, has not yet xeroxed his keester and faxed it to upper management.

FRIDAY: Inform him that "casual Friday" is actually "loincloth Friday."

Week Two: Alienating Him from His Colleagues

It's not enough that you dislike him. You have to make everybody *else* in the office loathe him as well. It's actually much easier than you might think, as long as you can keep a poker face and avoid anything that might resemble a guilty conscience.

MONDAY: Persuade him to spice up company e-mails with a little racy humor, adding "in bed" at the end of every sentence.

WEDNESDAY: Write a note that says, "We should work longer hours." Sign his name and drop it in the suggestion box.

FRIDAY: Tell him how much the boss enjoys jokes about his wife.

Week Three: The Nail in the Coffin

You're almost home free. Just a few more false moves and that gullible fool will have bought himself a one-way ticket to the Pink Slip Express. As long as he believes that you're the only one he can trust, he won't know what hit him.

MONDAY: Leave drug paraphernalia in his *To Do* box.

WEDNESDAY: Assure him that downloading pornography is not only allowed, it's encouraged.

FRIDAY: Invite him to root through the office supply cabinet and steal whatever he needs. Promptly call Security.

Chapter 4

Bossology

Types of Bosses

Bosses come in many shapes and sizes, and there are pros and cons to each. While some bosses may pass out pink slips like they're candy, others may have you serving a life sentence in middle management. Check out the following boss types and see how you can make the most of your situation.

The Tyrant Boss

HOW HE'LL MAKE YOUR LIFE HELL:

- May suddenly start firing people "just because."
- Thinks any problem can be fixed by screaming at it till it cries.
- Enjoys using pencils and staplers as projectile weapons.
- Has no sense of humor.

HOW HE'LL MAKE YOUR LIFE EASIER:

- Already assumes that you've screwed up, so there's no need to get it right the first time.
- May very well give himself a heart attack at any moment.
- His rage is easily deflected toward a less deserving coworker.
- Unlikely he'll realize you're making jokes about him.

The Paranoid Boss

HOW HE'LL MAKE YOUR LIFE HELL:

■ Is convinced that the company will go belly-up before lunch.

■ Can't make a decision without getting an opinion from everybody—including the janitor.

■ Perpetual sweating.

■ Will never, ever, *ever* give you a raise.

HOW HE'LL MAKE YOUR LIFE EASIER:

■ Too terrified to open his e-mail—using the logic that "the Internet is crawling with viruses"—so he's happy to be left out of the loop.

■ Make passing references to "your friend at the IRS" and you'll win instant job security.

■ Tell him, "I heard that the CEO is making a surprise visit," and he'll disappear for weeks.

■ Is more afraid of you than you are of him.

The Buddy Boss

HOW HE'LL MAKE YOUR LIFE HELL:

■ Has given everybody on his staff a pet name.

■ Will share intimate details of his personal life with you.

■ Enlists your help to play pranks on senior management.

Types of Bosses

- Wants to "hang out" after work, making it impossible to gossip about him with your coworkers.

HOW HE'LL MAKE YOUR LIFE EASIER:

- Can be coaxed into just about anything by saying, "Come on, be a pal."

- It's difficult to be intimidated by somebody who wants to begin meetings with a high five.

- Did he really agree to give you a huge salary hike after last night's fifth round of shots? Why yes, he certainly did.

- He can't fire a friend.

The Ancient Boss

HOW HE'LL MAKE YOUR LIFE HELL:

- Thinks that e-mail "is just a fad."

- Begins most sentences with, "Well, in *my* day . . ."

- Smells like talcum powder.

- Not sure why the women in his office don't like being called "dames."

HOW HE'LL MAKE YOUR LIFE EASIER:

- Impressed with your ability to operate a fax machine.

- Will accept "I came down with a nasty case of diphtheria" as a valid excuse for missing work.

■ Lost another major account for the company? Just ask him about his grandkids.

■ Will probably drop dead before too long.

The Missing Boss

HOW HE'LL MAKE YOUR LIFE HELL:

■ Unclear whether he's dead or just on sabbatical.

■ Thanks to his constant absence, his power-hungry secretary now has actual power.

■ Prefers interacting with his employees via a speakerphone, which has a creepy *Charlie's Angels* vibe.

■ You've forgotten what he looks like, so any unfamiliar face in the office must be approached with caution.

HOW HE'LL MAKE YOUR LIFE EASIER:

■ Doesn't remember your name, so you're unlikely to be reprimanded.

■ Can't verify just how much vacation time you've actually taken.

■ Will happily accept an excuse like, "Oh, that must've happened when you were away."

■ Your incompetence may go unnoticed for years.

Boss-to-English Translator: What Your Boss Says and What He Really Means

Do you ever feel a trip to your boss's office is like a trip to a foreign country? Nice view, but no speaka dee English? In order to ensure that none of the buck passing, put-downing, or one-upping is lost in translation, make sure to bring along this cheat sheet so you know what the big enchilada is really trying to say.

"Great job on the report!"

Translation: "I'm taking credit for your work."

"I have to attend an off-site meeting."

Translation: "I'm having an affair."

"Let me give you some broadstroke ideas and you can fill in the rest."

Translation: "I still haven't learned how to create an Excel document."

"Headquarters has assured me we will not be affected by the merger."

Translation: "You are going to be fired."

"I'm not sure if what you are suggesting is in alignment with our core competencies."

Translation: "What exactly do we do again?"

*"This office is a family and my door is always open
if you ever need to powwow with Papa Bear."*

Translation: "I am a tool."

*"I'll be out of the office for a couple
hours with senior management, but
you can reach me on my mobile."*

Translation: "I'm playing golf."

*"I'll be off-site and unreachable
for the rest of the afternoon."*

Translation: "I'm playing golf and I expect to be very, very drunk."

*"I think we should order in
some lunch for the team."*

Translation: "None of you are getting a raise. Enjoy your pizza."

*"I don't want to have to micromanage
this whole operation!"*

Translation: "I'm the boss because I made good business contacts at
my Ivy League university; I don't know how to actually do things."

"This came down from up top."

Translation: "I have no real power."

*"I can't give you an answer at this moment.
Let me survey the situation and see what
we can leverage out of it."*

Translation: "Oh God, I wish I was still in sales!"

Boss-to-English Translator

> *"It's good to see you take such bold initiative!"*
>> Translation: "You are a threat to me. You will be fired the
>> next time we so much as run out of coffee."

> *"I'll think about it."*
>> Translation: "I'll tell you no in an e-mail, long after I've left the office."

> *"Did you finish those projections I asked you
> about on Friday?"*
>> Translation: "I completely forgot to ask you about the projections
>> on Friday, and I'm hoping your memory is even worse than mine."

> *"This is a very sensitive issue."*
>> Translation: "I may need you to shred some documents."

> *"Let's push the boundaries on this one. We need
> something really innovative! Throw out the
> conventions, I want something edgy!"*
>> Translation: "Present only safe, traditional ideas to me. I wouldn't
>> know what to do with innovation if my life depended on it."

> *"We're going to be pulling some long hours and
> I'll be right here with the rest of you."*
>> Translation: "My home life is miserable."

> *"I hate to be the bearer of bad news."*
>> Translation: "Disappointing you is the only pleasure
>> I have left in my dead-end, crappy job."

Performance Evaluation

Evaluation Instructions

The evaluation form below will become part of the employee's permanent file, along with his or her elementary school report cards, high school art projects, dental records, and police rap sheet. The evaluation should be sprung on the employee on a yearly basis as a substitute for communication and coaching on your part throughout the rest of the year. Once the employee becomes comfortable with the evaluation process, the process should be changed.

Distribution Instructions

Supervisor and employee should sign the form and then make three copies. Return one copy to Human Resources, put your copy in the back of a drawer where you won't look at it again until next year, and give one copy to the employee to obsess over.

Evaluation Form

Employee Name _____ SS# _____

Employee Nickname _____
If none, skip. Or enter "Skip" as nickname.

Use a number 2 pencil to complete this form. If a number 2 pencil is not available, use two number 1 pencils. Clearly circle *a* or *b* after each subject heading. (If you need more instructions than this, should you really be supervising anyone?)

Performance Evaluation

QUALITY OF WORK ————————————————————

   a. Assigned projects seem finished.

   b. Projects seem as if they were just written in Finnish.

HOUSEKEEPING ————————————————————

   a. Employee's work area is neat and tidy.

   b. Work area looks like employee is expecting a visit from Grady and Lamont.

COMMUNICATIONS ————————————————————

   a. You find yourself hanging on employee's every word.

   b. You have thoughts of hanging the employee if someone gives the word.

TEAMWORK ————————————————————

   a. Employee stands out in a team.

   b. Employee is another faceless cog in the corporate machine who could be replaced at any time by another worker bee. (This is not necessarily a bad thing.)

Performance Evaluation

INITIATIVE

    a. Employee is a self-starter.

    b. Employee should be checked for a pulse daily.

JUDGMENT

    a. You can trust the employee's judgment consistently.

    b. You can trust the employee's judgment to be consistently wrong.

MULTITASKING

    a. Employee is comfortable handling a wide range of projects and responsibilities.

    b. Employee can be depended on to screw up one job at a time.

ATTENDANCE

    a. Employee is regularly at work and productive.

    b. When employee is out sick, office productivity actually goes up.

Performance Evaluation

LEADERSHIP
a. A natural-born leader?

b. First in line at the company picnic?

DELEGATION
a. Sensibly manages workload by proper delegation of nonessential tasks.

b. Loudly yells: "NOT IT!"

Rating Scale: Add one point for every *b* answer you circled.

9–11 points: *Unacceptable.* Dumb as a bag of hammers. Can barely summon up the mental electrical power to keep heart and lungs operating. Recommended for promotion.

7–8 points: *Needs improvement.* Warm body. Helps you meet your head count requirement, but not much more.

5–6 points: *Meets expectations.* As long as your expectations are really low.

3–4 points: *Exceeds expectations.* Doesn't accomplish any more than anyone else, but the constant apple polishing makes you feel like Donald Trump.

0–2 points: *Superior.* Bucking for your job. Must be destroyed.

How to Get Promoted: A Handy Flow Chart

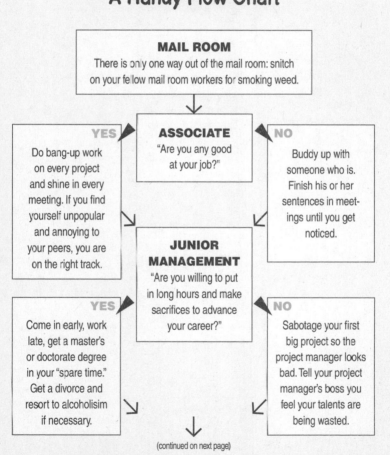

MAIL ROOM

There is only one way out of the mail room: snitch on your fellow mail room workers for smoking weed.

YES

Do bang-up work on every project and shine in every meeting. If you find yourself unpopular and annoying to your peers, you are on the right track.

ASSOCIATE

"Are you any good at your job?"

NO

Buddy up with someone who is. Finish his or her sentences in meetings until you get noticed.

JUNIOR MANAGEMENT

"Are you willing to put in long hours and make sacrifices to advance your career?"

YES

Come in early, work late, get a master's or doctorate degree in your "spare time." Get a divorce and resort to alcoholisim if necessary.

NO

Sabotage your first big project so the project manager looks bad. Tell your project manager's boss you feel your talents are being wasted.

(continued on next page)

How to Get Promoted: A Handy Flow Chart

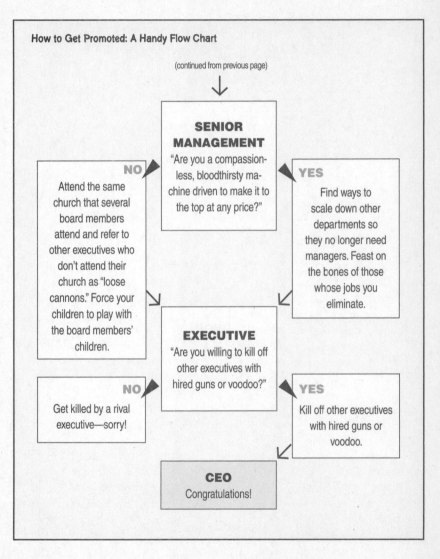

(continued from previous page)

SENIOR MANAGEMENT
"Are you a compassionless, bloodthirsty machine driven to make it to the top at any price?"

NO ► Attend the same church that several board members attend and refer to other executives who don't attend their church as "loose cannons." Force your children to play with the board members' children.

YES ► Find ways to scale down other departments so they no longer need managers. Feast on the bones of those whose jobs you eliminate.

EXECUTIVE
"Are you willing to kill off other executives with hired guns or voodoo?"

NO ► Get killed by a rival executive—sorry!

YES ► Kill off other executives with hired guns or voodoo.

CEO
Congratulations!

Are You an Ass Kisser?

Nobody wants to think that they're the office kiss-ass, but your actions speak louder than words. Take this quiz and find out just how brown your nose really is.

1. When your boss interrupts a company meeting with yet another lame joke, you . . .

❏ a. Ignore him.
❏ b. Smile politely and try not to roll your eyes.
❏ c. Laugh so hard you nearly give yourself an aneurysm.

2. Your screen saver is . . .

❏ a. A kitten hanging from a tree branch.
❏ b. Animated toasters with wings.
❏ c. The boss's family portrait.

3. Your coworkers have remarked that you'd make a great . . .

❏ a. Sales representative.
❏ b. Marketing director.
❏ c. Politician.

Are You an Ass Kisser?

Q

4. Your most common physical ailment is . . .

❏ a. Carpal tunnel syndrome.
❏ b. Backaches.
❏ c. Neck cramps from all the constant nodding.

5. You have, on at least one occasion . . .

❏ a. Complimented your boss on his appearance.
❏ b. Volunteered to stay late and finish work that wasn't your responsibility.
❏ c. Called your boss at 3 A.M. "just to make sure he's okay."

6. Your boss would describe you as . . .

❏ a. Motivated.
❏ b. A go-getter.
❏ c. Clingy.

7. At the end of a business day, you usually . . .

❏ a. Drive straight home to your family.
❏ b. Join your coworkers for a cocktail.
❏ c. Loiter in the parking lot, hoping to "accidentally" run into your boss and get invited to his house for dinner.

Are You an Ass Kisser?

8. You've been promoted to regional manager, despite
the fact that you . . .
- ❏ a. Have not expressed an interest.
- ❏ b. Have been with the company for only six weeks.
- ❏ c. Have no discernible talents.

SCORING: Give yourself three points for each question you answered *c*, and no points for each question you answered *a* or *b*.

0 points:	Congratulations! You've managed to keep your lips off the boss's tuckus. You may not get that big promotion, but at least you have your dignity.
3–15 points:	You're not a complete suck-up—you prob-ably think you're just being "motivationally affable"—but you're definitely heading in that direction.
18–30 points:	You are a sniveling toady with an insatiable lust for power. Everything you do and say has been carefully calculated to make the best impression, proving not only that you're the sole dependable employee, but the boss's best friend. See you in hell!

Screenplay:

"It Could Be Worse— The True Tale of a Boss from Hell"

<u>INT. CEO's OFFICE - MORNING</u>

We see the door close.

The CEO, a middle-aged man with thinning hair, sits at his desk, head in hands.

> CEO
> That was the tenth applicant
> we've had this week. I'm never
> going to fill this position.

The intercom buzzes and we hear the receptionist.

> RECEPTIONIST (v-o)
> Sir, I have a last-minute appli-
> cant for the position. A Mr. B.
> L. Zebub.

> CEO
> Well, send him in. What have I
> got to lose?

B. L. ZEBUB enters. He is an actual devil— horns, cloven hooves, and all—but dressed tastefully in a custom Italian suit.

The CEO waves B.L. to a guest chair. He sits.

> B. L. ZEBUB
> Thank you for seeing me on such
> short notice. I understand you
> have a position open?

> CEO
> Yes, in our Human Resources
> Department.

Close-up of B.L., lit from below, rubbing
his hands maniacally.

> B. L. ZEBUB
> Eeeex-cellent.

A bead of sweat rolls down the CEO's forehead. He wipes it away with a handkerchief
and collects himself.

> CEO
> I presume you have a résumé of
> some sort.

B. L. ZEBUB produces a weathered parchment
with the writing aflame.

> B. L. ZEBUB
> I think you'll find everything in
> order.

The CEO reads from the résumé.

It Could be Worse

                    CEO
          Positions held: Prince of Dark-
          ness. Ruler of the Underworld.
          Speechwriter for the Nixon admin-
          istration . . .

               B. L. ZEBUB
          There was a recession.

                    CEO
          Of course.

The CEO puts résumé down on his desk and
questions B.L.

                    CEO
          Let me ask you this: where do you
          see yourself in five years?

As B.L. outlines his plan, the office is suddenly transformed into the very pits of hell it-
self: fire, brimstone, the whole nine yards.

               B. L. ZEBUB
          I see a population enslaved and
          working in everlasting torment.
          Their only hope: a tomorrow that
          never comes. Instead they labor
          over meaningless tasks, such as
          pushing a boulder up a mountain
          only to have it crash impotently
          down the other side. Their only
          reward: to begin over again—over
          and over through an empty eternity.

We find ourselves suddenly back in the CEO's
office.

The CEO stares.

The CEO stands and shakes hands with B.L.

> CEO
> (smiling broadly)
> Sounds good! About time we got
> some order around here. And your
> salary requirement?

> B. L. ZEBUB
> I shall require twelve human souls
> a year.

> CEO
> Six.

> B. L. ZEBUB
> Nine. And not a soul less.

The CEO contemplates this for a moment, then
gives a quick nod of his head.

> CEO
> Done! You're a shrewd bargainer.

CEO shakes B.L.'s hand and escorts him toward the door.

> B. L. ZEBUB
> I'm the best!

> THE END

Prescripted E-Mails to Your Boss

Picking up the phone or leaving your chair to talk to a colleague is so 1991. These days, giving orders or passing the blame is as simple as pecking away on a keyboard. A perfectly scripted e-mail can get you a deadline extension, a raise, or a permanent place in your boss's good graces. If you're not much of a writer, don't worry: we've made e-mailing as easy as copy-and-paste.

TO: BOSS
SUBJECT: PROJECT UPDATE

Due to unforeseen economic conditions last quarter, I will need to revise my budget numbers to better reflect the overall hostile climate toward capital investment vis-à-vis the Boolean projection model used to forecast Six Sigma compliance.

This is the Emperor's New Clothes of e-mails. It doesn't actually say anything, but your boss will be too intimidated to admit he doesn't understand it.

TO: BOSS
SUBJECT: OUT OF THE OFFICE

This Friday I will be out of the office doing charitable work with the Lepers, Wid-
ows, and Orphans Society of America and
will be unable to check my e-mail . . .

*. . . because they don't have a Wi-Fi connection at
the Nordstrom shoe sale.*

TO: BOSS
SUBJECT: FW: JOB OFFER

Pursuant to our conversation last week, we
would like to offer you a salary $10,000
above what you are making in your current position. We understand the intense
loyalty you expressed toward your current
employers, but unless they can match this
offer, shouldn't you consider your own
interests first?
    Hoping to hear from you soon.
    GloboCorp

*"Accidentally" forward this e-mail to your boss
when annual pay increases are being decided upon.*

Are You an Ass Kisser?

TO: BOSS
SUBJECT: OFFICE HOURS

Just checking if the office will be open this weekend. I want to start some new projects that lie outside my assigned duties, but I don't want to encroach on my regular work hours.

File under U for "unadulterated crap."

TO: BOSS
SUBJECT: SPAM FILTERS

We need to get IT to install some more aggressive spam filters. The spreadsheet that I had ready for today's sales meeting has been corrupted by the Trojan Worm virus that is going around and I have to start all over again.
　　Aaargh!

This should buy you another day.

Nobody Likes Me: Headlines on Famous Indicted Bosses

While bosses have distinct personalities and management styles, there is one trait that lands them all in the big kahuna genus: they're all suckers for the limelight. Find out how these famous bosses made headlines.

1338.

Disgraced Samurai Warrior Nitta Yoshisada Chops Off Own Head, Expects Entire Army to Do Same. "Whatever, Dude," Says Former General, Who Opts to Sudoku.

1876.

GEORGE CUSTER LEADS U.S. CAVALRY INTO BATTLE WITH AMERICAN INDIANS, RESULTING IN SLAUGHTER. CUSTER'S "WORLD'S BEST BOSS" COFFEE MUG REVOKED.

Nobody Likes Me: Headlines on Famous Indicted Bosses

1887.

Corrupt Industrialist George Pullman Slashes Employee Wages, Cuts Jobs. Surprised When Nobody Attends Birthday Party.

1929.

MOB BOSS AL CAPONE MASTER-MINDS KILLING OF 7 IN RIVAL GANG IN ST. VALENTINE'S DAY MASSACRE, CALLS IT "CORPORATE DOWNSIZING."

1941.

NEWSPAPER TYCOON WILLIAM RANDOLPH HEARST ANGERED BY PORTRAYAL IN ORSON WELLES FILM "CITIZEN KANE."

Hearst's Staff Equally Incensed, Citing Lack of References to Hearst's Horns and "Fondness for Eating Babies."

Nobody Likes Me: Headlines on Famous Indicted Bosses

1957.

Reclusive Billionaire Howard Hughes Fires Entire Staff. Replaces Them with a Box of Tissues. Former Employees Strangely Relieved by News.

1989.

HOTEL HEIRESS LEONA HELMSLEY SENT TO PRISON FOR TAX EVASION, PROMISES TO "KEEP COT WARM" FOR MARTHA STEWART.

2007.

DONALD TRUMP KICKS OFF SIXTH SEASON OF HIT SHOW "THE APPRENTICE." Is Surprised in the Boardroom When His Hairpiece Is Named New CEO of Trump Enterprises. Wig Fires Trump, Laughs Sinisterly.

Chapter 5

Excuses for Everything

Fake Doctors' Notes

You were supposed to be at the office six hours ago. You just woke up with a blinding headache and a vague recollection of belting out "If you like piña coladas" on karaoke at 3 A.M. It's too late to call in sick and the boss will be furious. No cause for alarm. Just show up the next day with one of these bona fide doctor's notes and bask in the instantaneous sympathy bestowed upon you.

Please excuse *(insert your name)* from work yesterday. He/she required an emergency blood transfusion for a severe paper cut inflicted while retrieving a Starburst from the recycling bin.

(Insert your name) was not in due to extreme chafing around the wrists from chains on his/her desk.

Please excuse *(insert your name)*'s absence. He/she was admitted to our emergency room for smoke inhalation from burnt popcorn in the microwave.

Please take it easy on *(insert your name)* this week. He/she broke an arm yesterday while wrestling over the last box of Kleenex in the supply room—which I understand are traded in your office much like cigarettes are traded in prison.

Please excuse *(insert your name)* from work indefinitely as he/she is suffering from hysterical blindness. The affliction came on when *(insert your name)* realized that he/she accidentally hit "reply all" in an e-mail discussing the resemblance of the boss's new baby to the UPS man.

Game: Blame the Temp!

Here's a fun and educational game for the whole office. And best of all, it's free!

THE OBJECT: Each player chooses a real temp from around the office. Be the first to get your temp fired and you win!

EQUIPMENT: You will need one temp for each player. (If your office has cut back on hiring paid temp workers, interns may be substituted.)

RULES: There are no rules except "Eat or Be Eaten."

STRATEGY: "Positive Game Moves" should be used to help you get that all-important pink slip for your temp. But be careful! Some game moves may backfire. And remember, if you get fired yourself, you lose—your job, your house, your significant other. It's a dangerous game we're playing here. But you'll never feel so alive!

Positive Game Moves

- Start stealing little things around the office the same day your temp starts.
- Tell the temp the reserved parking spaces are totally cool to park in.
- Steal temp's temporary clip-on ID pass and replace with card reading "Free Butt Massages."
- Place pamphlet titled *Eliminating Head Lice* sticking out of temp's purse or pocket.
- Get application from temp's agency online. Leave it jammed in the printer.
- Arrive to work late. Insist temp had offered to pick you up the day before.

Game: Blame the Temp!

■ Doctor temp's time sheet so she claims to have worked 128 hours that week.

■ Convince temp that hitting "delete" saves work to the master database.

■ Temp falls for "Tomorrow's Flag Day; no work!"

■ Anonymously send temp box of laxative-laced chocolates. Suggest she pass them around the office to make new friends.

Game Moves That Backfired

■ You make fun of temp's ugly sweater, then she explains it was given to her by Darfur refugees whom she helped while working in the Peace Corps.

■ Temp reorganizes filing system you've been sabotaging.

■ In front of crowd, attempt to embarrass temp by asking her how long it's been since she's had any real employment. She comes back with, "How long have you had your menial desk job?"

■ While digging for dirt in the temp's HR file you discover temp has master's degree from Yale.

■ To beat a deadline, have temp write a report, then hand it in as your own. In your boss's office you discover the temp likes to use the F-word in reports.

■ Steal temp's lunch. Discover she is a vegan.

■ Attempt to send temp infected file. She develops a firewall that is now used officewide.

■ Make fun of temp's alma mater in front of boss. Realize boss went to same school as temp.

■ Send temp on an office wild-goose chase. She bumps into old school friend, who is now a VP.

■ While temp is away from desk, go to her computer and log on an Internet gambling site. She comes back and wins $5,000.

Excuse Mad Libs

Fill in the blanks and redirect the blame like a pro!

Your Project Is Overdue

I would have completed the _____ project on
Anglo-Saxon surname

time, but _____ didn't get me the _____
name of intern<space>buzzword randomly taken

report in a timely manner, so I was unable
out of *Wall Street Journal*

to put the data into _____. I should be able
unreliable software product

to get it no later than _____, unless, of
date randomly picked from calendar

course, _____ drops the _____.
another department in company<space>piece of sports equipment

You're Late for Work

I would have been here earlier, but my
name of kitchen appliance

broke down this morning and you know how I need

my type of food or drink or I'm a zombie. And then while I was

driving on name of major freeway a type of vehicle rolled over and

dumped a load of name of farm animals all over the road. Then

the guys from name of government agency came in for the cleanup

and you know how they are, like a
name of different farm animal

in a type of store . But thank name of deity I'm here now, safe

and sound.

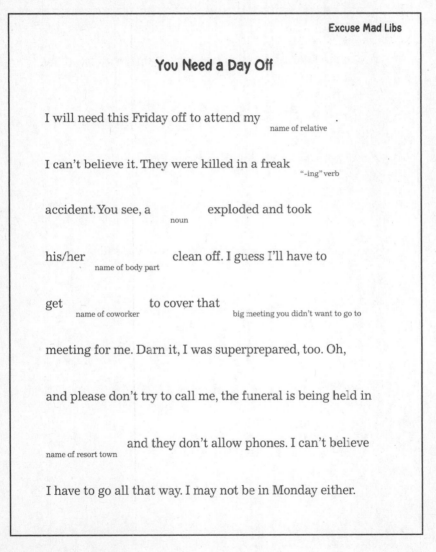

Excuse Mad Libs

You Need a Day Off

I will need this Friday off to attend my _____.
name of relative

I can't believe it. They were killed in a freak _____
"-ing" verb

accident. You see, a _____ exploded and took
noun

his/her _____ clean off. I guess I'll have to
name of body part

get _____ to cover that _____
name of coworker   big meeting you didn't want to go to

meeting for me. Darn it, I was superprepared, too. Oh,

and please don't try to call me, the funeral is being held in

_____ and they don't allow phones. I can't believe
name of resort town

I have to go all that way. I may not be in Monday either.

Excuse Mad Libs

You Incited a Class-Action Lawsuit Against the Company

I can explain everything. You see the _____ has really
name of government agency

been cracking down on companies ever since the

_____ scandal. It was in the _____, so
name of Fortune 500 company   name of major newspaper

I'm sure you know all about it. Anyway, my designs for _____
name of product

weren't in compliance with the _____
random combination of letters and numbers

regulations passed by the _____ legislature last year. But if
name of state

I'm going down, I'm taking you with me. I have compromising

photos of you and _____ in the _____ doing the
name of sexy coworker   name of local sleazy motel

_____ with a _____. Do we understand each other?
name of embarrassing act   type of vegetable

Excuses for Coming In Late
for Chronic Offenders

Late to the office again? No problem! Use the "Excuse-O-Meter" to come up with the perfect explanation for your tardiness. Just make one selection from each column and you'll have an excuse that's guaranteed to work (or at least confuse your boss) every time.

I would have made it to work on time, but . . .

My spouse . . .	. . . swallowed my car keys.
My cat . . .	. . . slipped a roofie into my coffee.
A hired assassin . . .	. . . went into labor.
My neighbor . . .	. . . was weeping hysterically.
A rogue gang of bikers . . .	. . . says I'm contagious. Here, feel.
My attorney . . .	. . . just needed "to talk."
My elderly grandmother . . .	. . . stuck a potato in my exhaust pipe.
The FBI . . .	. . . came to me in a dream and told me to sleep in.
My doctor . . .	. . . got into the crawl space.
The client . . .	. . . needed an organ donation.
God . . .	. . . refused to untie me.

How to Get Away with Missed Deadlines, Getting Caught Sleeping at the Job, or Anything Else

Nothing is against office policy if you don't get caught doing it. In case you do, here are some handy tips to get you out of trouble.

MISSING A DEADLINE. Show up to the office several days later, with a shaved head and tattered clothes, muttering, "You're not gonna *believe* what happened to me."

SLEEPING AT YOUR DESK. Claim that you have narcolepsy. To confirm your story, begin randomly falling asleep at the most inconvenient (and occasionally physically dangerous) moments, like while pouring coffee or using the paper shredder.

USING THE OFFICE COPIER FOR PERSONAL DOCUMENTS. Feign confusion. Didn't the client request three hundred copies of your family Christmas letter? Say something nebulous like, "Yeah, I thought that was kinda weird, too," and promise to follow up on it.

SNOOPING THROUGH SOMEONE ELSE'S DESK. You could've sworn that you saw a huge rat run into his cubicle.

In the confusion, recommend that the entire staff get rabies shots, "just to be safe."

▦

USING THE OFFICE COMPUTER TO SHOP ONLINE. It must be a computer glitch. You've been trying to access the client's Web site for hours, but it keeps redirecting you to the Target checkout page. Promise to call tech support "after lunch."

✉

EATING SOMEONE ELSE'S LUNCH. Spread a rumor about anthrax poisoning. Insist that the boss asked you to eat anything in the employee fridge that might be contaminated. Say, "I guess I'm just expendable," before breaking down into violent sobs.

☏

IGNORING THE DRESS CODE. Using Photoshop, create the cover of a faux fashion magazine, featuring a picture of someone in sweats and the heading "New Office Chic." Refer to the cover when questioned.

◔

SMOKING AT YOUR CUBE. Allege that it's medical marijuana.

🗀

Chapter 6

Meeting Schmetiquette

I've Got No Agenda Here: An All-Purpose Meeting Agenda Template

Let's face it, you go to hundreds of pointless meetings every year. And after a while, they all start to run together. It helps to have an agenda at these meetings, but these don't always get followed the way they should. Below is a meeting agenda that conforms to the way meetings in corporate America are *really* run.

MEETING AGENDA

❑ Search for the minutes from the previous meeting.

❑ Reading of the minutes from the previous meeting.

❑ Tabling of the reading of the minutes from the previous meeting.

❑ Boy, the traffic was hell this morning.

❑ Confirm all chocolate glazed doughnuts are gone.

❑ Weather report.

❑ Update on outstanding projects.

❑ Budget number projections.

❑ Excuses for being over budget.

❑ PowerPoint presentation on . . . oh, who really gives a rip?

❑ Where does this cord need to go to get the PowerPoint presentation working?

❑ Anyone see any good movies?

❑ Who stepped on a duck?

❑ Delegating work to subordinates.

❑ Speculate on the size of the next round of bonuses.

❑ Discussing health-care-benefits cutbacks.

❑ Handouts (bring one less than the number of attendees).

❑ What's everyone doing this weekend?

❑ Setting a date and time for the next meeting.

Beyond Pie: Innovative Charts
They Haven't Seen Before

Do your presentations mean a one-way ticket to Snoozeville for the listeners? Well, the cause may not be you (okay, it may be you). But it could also be a case of not having the right graphics to explain the company's current situation or spice up the topic at hand. Check out the following alternative charts designed to capture your audience's attention and keep their nap time to a minimum.

CAKE CHART. "For those who don't like pie."

PIE CHART (WITH AN EXTRA SLICE). "When you're over budget and need a little extra dough."

BAR CHART. "When you'd rather be at the bar than at another PowerPoint presentation."

DISORGANIZATIONAL CHART. "Shows how the organization *really* works."

BLOOD PRESSURE CHART. "You, if you have to look at one more &%*#ing chart."

Top Ten Snappy Responses and Quick Recoveries to Questions You Didn't Hear Because You Were Zoned Out

1. "I'm not going to dignify that with a response!"

2. "Whoa, I just had one of my psychic realizations: someone in this room is embezzling money!"

3. "What did you say about my wife!?" They will quickly repeat the question.

4. Raise your index finger to your lips and say, "Shhh, let's all just listen with our hearts for a moment. I think the answer will become obvious."

5. "I must have answered this question a hundred times in the last month! Doesn't anybody listen anymore?"

6. Act as if you are silently falling in love with the person waiting for your response.

7. Act as if you are going to respond, then pause to reconsider your response. Repeat for hours on end until quitting time.

8. Hang your head and say, "What difference does it make? We're all going to die anyway!"

9. "That may be true. Or not. What do you think, Ed?"

10. "I didn't hear your question; I zoned out. I was a million miles away. Which brings up a greater issue: what are we going to do to liven up these lame meetings?"

Great Moments in Meeting History

MARCH 23, 1775. At a meeting of American patriots in Richmond, Virginia, Patrick Henry delivers his famous speech, declaring, "Give me liberty or give me death." He goes on to overexplain this "liberty-or-death proposal" with a PowerPoint demonstration, causing at least a few in attendance to exclaim, "We get it already." After four hours, a vote is passed to order pizza.

MAY 1, 1867. The Bavarian Illuminati, the infamous secret society of freemasons, hold their first meeting. "Action items" in the agenda include conspiring to control international affairs, picking world leaders to act in a puppet regime, and implementing a "fancy new design" for the society's letterhead.

FEBRUARY 11, 1945. Churchill, Roosevelt, and Stalin attend a historic meeting in Soviet Union to sign the Yalta accord. Stalin is granted complete sovereignty over most of Eastern Europe in exchange for providing vouchers for the Moscow Marriott Hotel and unlimited coffee for United Nations meetings.

APRIL 23, 1956. Due to poor planning, a company meeting at Leonard & Associates in New York drags on for twenty-three days and eleven minutes, breaking the record for longest meeting in business history. The survivors, who are airlifted to Mount Sinai

Great Moments in Meeting History

for malnutrition and acute boredom, later admit to
succumbing to cannibalism. Surprisingly, they also
admit to eating "James from Accounting" after just
three hours, mostly because he was a long-winded
ass.

FEBRUARY 1971–JULY 1973. U.S. president Richard Nixon
secretly records over three thousand hours of White
House meetings. The tapes are subpoenaed during
the Watergate scandal, and eighteen minutes are
mysteriously missing. Nixon insists that the lost
tapes mostly consisted of him and Kissinger telling
blond jokes, which really weren't that funny in the
first place.

JUNE 2, 2007. Robert Dickenson, promotions director
at an Internet start-up, is overheard uttering the
following sentence during a marketing meeting:
"I think we need to integrate some synergistic func-
tionalities and be more proactive about streamlining
our strategic initiatives in real time without forgetting to leverage our paradigms with leading-edge
and magnetic infomediaries, with respect to the ex-
isting infrastructures." Although none of his associates has any idea what he's talking about, it marks
the first instance in which a staggering ten obsequi-
ous buzzwords are used in a single sentence.

Step-by-Step Guide to Get You
Out of the Meeting from Hell

What constitutes the "meeting from hell"? Nobody listening to you, everyone going in circles, no one addressing the real issues, management ignoring the efforts you've made. It's a twenty-year bad marriage crammed into three hours. But no need to suffer through it. Just follow these simple steps to get out of a meeting.

STEP ONE **IDENTIFY.** Ask yourself this simple question: if a rusty saw blade were made available, would I attempt to cut my own head off? If the answer is yes, it's time to put the wheels of escape into motion.

STEP TWO **PLANT THE SEED.** Tell the group you have a horrible feeling you've forgotten something. Discreetly but obviously double-check that you are wearing pants. Once your point is made shrug your shoulders and say, "Oh well, it will come to me." Move immediately to Step Three.

STEP THREE **CALL THE CAVALRY.** Send a text message to the office manager asking her to send a car for your supervisor (we'll call her Jill), who is also attending

Step-by-Step Guide to Get You Out of the Meeting from Hell

the meeting. Tell the office manager that Jill has to go to the airport for an emergency meeting with a huge client (we'll call him McDoogle) and is to be personally notified the moment the car arrives. Silently pray Jill is as cool as you think.

STEP FOUR

STRIKE. When the office manager interrupts to announce the car arrived to take Jill to the airport, Jill will, of course, be confused and ask, "Why am I going to the airport?" The office manager will say, "For that emergency McDoogle meeting!" That's when you spring into action: that's what you were forgetting! Grab Jill by the arm and tell her you'll give her a full briefing on the way to the airport.

STEP FIVE

CAPITALIZE ON AN OPPORTUNITY. Once Jill is in the car, be straight with her and tell her exactly what you've done. Chances are she wanted to get out of that meeting just as bad as you did. If she is upset and threatens disciplinary action, buy her a big cinnamon roll, a $9 beer, and put her in one of those massage chairs when you get to the airport. She'll calm down.

How to Turn a Meeting into a Drinking Game

Stuck in another pointless midday meeting? Turn it into a drinking game and you'll be too soused to care that your time is being needlessly wasted! Here are some simple rules to get you started.

⊛When somebody describes his idea as "proactive" even though it is clearly neither "pro" nor "active," **take a drink**.

⊛When an idea is described as "magnetic" despite its inability to attract iron or steel, **take a drink**.

⊛When the team leader refers to him- or herself in the plural ("We believe this is a good course of action"), **take a drink**.

⊛When two annoying buzzwords are combined to make a new, meaningless buzzword such as "incentivization" or "paradigmovation," **take a drink**.

⊛When a coworker says, "Good point," even before the boss finishes his sentence, **take a drink**.

⊛When a coworker announces that she has to leave early for "an important business call with a client," **make her take a drink**.

⊛When bullet points are used in a presentation, **take a drink for each bullet**.

⊛When somebody suggests "thinking outside the box" and is not referring to mimes, **take a drink**.

⊛When the prefix "e" is added to a word, such as "e-business" or "e-commerce" or "e-markets," **take a "virtual" drink**.

⊛When somebody comes up with a ridiculous metaphor meant to be both motivational and cute—such as "I want to stir-fry some ideas in your brain-wok"—**take a drink**.

⊛When the prefix "re" is added to a word, such as "recontextualize" or "redefine" or "reintermediate," **poke a hole in the bottom of your cup and drink from the leak**.

⊛When somebody uses the phrase "Take it to the next level," **finish the bottle**.

Chapter 7

Small Talk

Schmooze Your Way to the Top: Great Conversation Starters at Company Get-Togethers

Nothing says "carefully observed behavior and strict unspoken adherence to hierarchy" better than a corporate party. Here are a few icebreakers to keep things swinging at your next office gathering:

66 Doesn't this place look great? The crepe paper and streamers almost make me forget I want to kill myself. 99

66 I can't believe a party can be so much fun without prostitutes! 99

66 I know what this party needs; a little crazy fill-in-the-blanks Mad Lib game using an Excel spreadsheet! 99

66 I love your shoes, Mr. Watson. Who tied them for you? 99

66 Boy, I wish there was someone selling pacifiers and glow sticks here! 99

66 Thanks for throwing such a swell party, Ms. Reynolds. It's great to see your disdain for underlings in a purely social setting. 99

66 I wish my little dog Chester was here. He'd pee on the floor and leave like I wish I had the guts to. 99

❝This reminds me of the time I was forced into an awkward social situation with a bunch of people I shared no common interests with and secretly thought myself superior to—funny!❞

❝Hey! Khakis, a company golf shirt, and lanyard? I'm wearing khakis, a company golf shirt, and lanyard, too!❞

❝Anybody feel like doing some team-building exercises just for fun?❞

❝I believe current enjoyment levels are exceeding the projected forecasts.❞

❝I know some people were upset when we lost our 401(k) plan, but we wouldn't have been able to swing cake *and* chips at this party if we kept it.❞

❝Hey, everybody, I brought Trivial Pursuit: The Remedial-Questions-for-Corporate-Drones-Whose-Brains-Have-Atrophied-from-Lack-of-Use Edition. Who wants to play?!❞

❝We've worked together for six years, so this is a little awkward, but . . . what is your name again?❞

❝Boy, I really hate these things. Not corporate get-togethers. I mean, conversations with you.❞

Buttons That Let 'Em Know
What's Really on Your Mind

Sometimes you just can't summon up the energy to talk to the idiots in your office. Tape these phrases on handy buttons to save you the effort.

Decaffeinated.
Come back
in an hour.

Sexual
Harassment
Lawsuit Just
Waiting to
Happen

I Covered Up
Evidence of the
Boss's Tax Evasion
and All I Got Was
This Lousy
Button!

The
Company
Loves
Misery

Ask Me
About My
Useless
Philosophy
Degree

51%
Sweet
49%
Bee-otch

Hostile
Takeover?
*Not unless you
buy me dinner
first . . .*

Fax
THIS!

Spineless
Toady in
Training

*I'm Late
for
Something*

Defusing the Loaded Question

It's happened to all of us: a coworker asks a question that you're unable to answer because of either lack of preparation or complete ineptitude. Here are some ready-made responses for when you just don't have a clue.

1. "I suppose I could just tell you. But the only way you're going to learn is if you figure it out yourself."

2. *(In Yoda voice.)* "Path to the dark side, fear is. Fear leads to anger. Anger leads to hate. Hate leads to suffering."

3. "Do you know I can kill a man using only my pinkie?"

4. "Now, are you just asking me because you're trying to distract people from realizing that you've been embezzling money from the company for the past twelve years? Oh wait, was I not supposed to say that out loud?"

5. "Uhhh . . . okay, I can get this. First word. Sounds like . . . refrigerator? No. Marmoset? No. Aw hell, I used to be so good at charades."

6. "Oh, that's rich. You blatantly ignore my every request to be your MySpace friend, and now you're acting like we're best buddies when you need something from me. How *convenient*."

7. *(Long pause.)* "Oh, you wanted me to answer that? I thought you were just speaking rhetorically."

8. "Excellent question! I was hoping someone would ask that! Well done! I'm taking lunch!"

9. *(In hushed tone.)* "SHHHH! Don't let the boss hear you ask that! Do you want to get us all fired?"

10. "Look in your heart; I think you'll find the answer there."

Awards: Backhanded Compliments They'll Thank You For

In business it's important to celebrate achievements, even if those "achievements" are actually crippling character flaws. Here are a few examples of how to honor the dishonorable. They're people too, you know.

THE WEEKEND WORRIER AWARD
—awarded to the person most likely to dread repercussions of things said or done after too many margaritas at Chi-Chi's Friday happy hour

PERSONAL BEST AWARD
—given to the individual who will most likely never get another promotion

SENIOR MANAGEMENT PROJECTED ANONYMITY AWARD
—awarded to the manager most likely to refer to people he's worked with for years as "Lady" or "Big Guy"

GOLDEN THUMB AWARD
—given for spending an entire meeting texting someone outside the room

BEST DELIVERY AT A CLIENT PITCH (WITH FLY OPEN)

Awards: Backhanded Compliments They'll Thank You For

Most Likely
to Succeed
*(at a different
position)*

THE NOT-SO-GRIM REAPER AWARD
—awarded posthumously to
the employee whose death
went virtually unnoticed

THE WALK OF SHAME AWARD
—awarded to the employee who has
come in to work wearing the same
clothes two days in a row most often

THE FURRY FASHION AWARD
—awarded to the employee who
shows up most consistently
covered with pet hair

THE RISING STAR AWARD
—for the employee most likely
to appear on *Cops*.

THE "WE SHOULD HAVE SEEN IT COMING" AWARD
—awarded to the employee whose cubicle
decorations are most obviously a cry for help

THE 'ROID RAGE AWARD
—awarded to the employee who gets most
angry about losing the office football pool

Tone Deaf: Out-of-Office Voice Mail Messages They'll Never Forget

We all leave messages on other people's voice mail and we all know to leave our name and number and wait for the beep. So how are you going to make your outgoing message stand out from the crowd? Here are some original messages to help you out.

Hi, this is Jane. I'm in the office, I'm at my desk, I'm not on the other line. I just don't feel like talking to you.

☎

In addition to a message, please leave your Social Security number, your mother's maiden name, and a valid credit card number. Your identity will be stolen before the end of the day.

☎

How did you get this number? Did that jerk in Accounting give it to you? Well listen, I don't know what he told you, but I am *not* available for bachelor parties.

☎

Hi, this is Kenny. *(In a lower voice:)* And Peter. *(In a high voice:)* And Lady Bixby. *(In a regular voice:)* I have multiple personality disorder not covered by my company's HMO. If you leave a message, I'll just confuse it with the other voices in

Tone Deaf: Out-of-Office Voice Mail Messages They'll Never Forget

my head, so don't bother. *(In a lower voice:)* I knew you'd say that. *(In a regular voice:)* Shut up, Peter!

Don't bother leaving me a message. By the time you hear this, I'll be halfway to the border. And then I'll be free, do you hear me? Free!

My voice mailbox is full. But please leave a message anyway. Odds are, I wouldn't have listened to it anyway.

Hello? *(Long pause.)* Hello? *(Another long pause.)* Is anybody there? *(Another long pause.)* If this is some kind of joke, it isn't funny.

I'm out of the office today, but I'll be able to pick up your messages on my PDA. Yep, never out of touch, twenty-four/seven. God, I hate my life.

Gina, if this is you, I'm sorry for what I did. Interoffice romances are so awkward. It was the first time for me and I was nervous. I'm sure your cat will recover. If this is anyone else, please leave a message.

Famous Quotes

Saying something yourself means nothing. But repeating something someone else once said gives a real sense of legitimacy. Here are a few "quotes" that might help you get out of a jam. When asked who you're quoting say either, "That's what they say," or, "George Bernard Shaw."

"A project turned in late is a project turned in great!"

"Nothing cures underachievement faster than a raise."

"If you want to raise profits, first raise bonuses."

Famous Quotes

"*Drinking on the job is thinking on the job!*"

"Taking credit for an idea makes it your own."

"The customer is always right. Unless they're a complete moron."

"Coffee fuels the wheels of industry."

"If you're not part of the solution, there's money to be made in prolonging the problem."

How to Jazz Up Your E-Mail

Interoffice e-mails can be so unnecessarily boring. Here are some ways to spice up your e-mails and entertain your coworkers on company time.

1. Begin the e-mail with an informal greeting like "Dear Jerkface" or "This one goes out to all my business associates in lockup."
2. Write the entire e-mail in a nonsense font like Webdings. Label it "IMPORTANT."
3. Finish every sentence—particularly those containing bad news (like cuts to the company's health insurance plan)—with a smiley-face emoticon.
4. Compose your e-mail in iambic pentameter. Change potentially vital information to fit the meter.
5. Add random question marks, particularly when you're not asking a question: "I need to see the numbers on the Johnson account immediately?"
6. Include erroneous contact info for client (1-800-HOT-LIPS).
7. Sell ad space in your e-mails to competing companies. "Today's accounting report is brought to you by Joe's House of Wieners, where everyone hot dogs it."
8. Translate your e-mail into Snoop-Dogg-ese: "We will be implement'n new strategies ta grizzay participizzles in playa ta maximize interaction wit da clientizzle."
9. Claim to be the dignitary of a Nigerian government. Kindly request the use of the recipient's bank account by which to funnel your family fortune.
10. End all e-mails with the warning "This message will self-destruct in thirty seconds."

Chapter 8

In Case of Emergency

FEMA's Not Coming:
Match the Fix with the Disaster

Are you the type of person who can keep her cool while everyone else is panicking? If so, you are either a good leader or just unaware of your surroundings. To see how you would handle yourself in a disaster, take this simple quiz.

DISASTER

1. Your PowerPoint presentation freezes two slides into a major sales pitch. ____.

2. You break a nail. ____.

3. Fire in the office. ____.

4. Airport delays keep you from a big meeting. ____.

5. Blackout. ____.

6. Freak snowstorm strands you at office overnight. ____.

FIX

A. Slam hand in laptop. Insist you need to go immediately to the emergency room. Go get a manicure instead.

B. Remain motionless to avoid being noticed by predators. If possible, change colors so that you blend into your surroundings.

C. Walk around office with arms outstretched. Make the most of situation by "accidentally" hitting or groping various coworkers.

D. Ransack the office and people's personal items for any resources that could prove valuable.

E. Break out emergency office puppets. Use them to inform and entertain.

F. Pretend you are a traveling foreign dignitary and try to score with people sitting near you.

Hide and Seek: Advance Avoidance
Techniques for the 4:59 P.M. Assignment

It's almost 5 P.M. and you're ready to hear that metaphorical whistle blow and slide down the purple brontosaurus just like Fred Flintstone. But before you can say "Yabba-dabba-doo," your boss drops off "a quick little project." Looks like you're gonna end up staying late again . . . *unless* you're armed with these advanced work avoidance techniques:

GET THE STOMACH FLU. Making a bathroom run is only a temporary distraction. But announcing that you have irritable bowel syndrome is guaranteed to give you complete privacy for the rest of the day.

PUNT. You can avoid any extra work by "punting" to your cubicle mate. For example: "OSHA compliance? Ken is the expert on that topic. Why don't you tell the boss what you were telling me, Ken?"

STOP, DROP, AND ROLL. With no explanation, drop to the floor and begin rolling down the hallway. Continue rolling until you're in the parking lot.

HIDE. Bring your nephew to the office on a Saturday and play a game of hide-and-seek. You'll amass a great list of hiding spots that would have never occurred to you. Just don't lock yourself in one of those long file drawers next time your boss is looking for you. Ever wonder where Jenny in Accounting went . . . ?

START A FIRE. Not a big, life-threatening one, mind you. Just an oily-rags-in-the-garage type of fire to create a diversion while you slip out the back door.

ACT CRAZY. As a last resort, just mumble something vaguely insane. Complain that you can't open the Odessa File on your tape dispenser. Gaze out the window and mutter, "The gods are angry today." Enjoy the quiet inner satisfaction that you feel as your boss slowly backs away . . .

Time for Me to Fly: Coping with an Annoying Coworker on a Cross-Country Flight

What could possibly be worse than being trapped for eight hours in the same office with an annoying jerk-bag coworker? Being stuck on a four-hour flight with said jerk bag; and that's not counting airport delays! Here are some tips to make the flight from hell go more smoothly.

- The lavatory is a tailor-made personal cone of silence. Just ignore that pounding at the door and flush every five minutes to offer hope to your distressed cabin mates.
- If the small talk is going nowhere, put in the ear buds from your iPod and tell your coworker you're learning a foreign language for college credit. Close your eyes and quietly repeat foreign phrases like *E Pluribus Unum* and *Macarena.*
- Open up the overhead compartment, take out your carry-on bag, and pummel him in the head with it until he passes out. Later, explain, "Boy, they're not kidding when they say some shifting of the contents may occur during the flight."
- Look out the window and say, "I can see my house from here . . . I can still see it . . . Wait, I can still see it . . . I see it . . ." Continue this throughout the entire flight.
- Start randomly writing numbers on your cocktail napkin, concentrating intently. If he asks what you're doing, explain you're calculating the number of people you have to knock off to become CEO.
- Feign a rare form of paralysis, which is induced only by eating tiny pretzels. "The doctors are baffled, but it's my cross to bear." And then sleep . . . sleep.

Coupons: In Case You Forgot to Get a Gift for Betty's Surprise Party

You walk into the office, deep in thought, calculating how much longer you have to wait until lunchtime—blissfully unaware of what awaits you. You open the door and . . . SURPRISE! It's Betty's birthday . . . or Administrative Assistant's Day . . . or Arbor Day. And you are without a gift. Well, not anymore, Bunkie. Below are coupons that will save you from even the most arcane gift-giving occasion. Enjoy!

Good for
helping you find a document you swear got mysteriously deleted!

You're going to end up doing it anyway, right?

FREE
French Fries

Valid only in France

Coupons: In Case You Forgot to Get a Gift for Betty's Surprise Party

ONE-WAY TRIP TO SIBERIA

Come on. Can't you think of someone you'd love to give this to?

ONE TEXT MESSAGE
sent to you during
a meeting of
YOUR CHOOSING

So you can appear important, too

ONE
show of support for
ASININE IDEA

Perfect for boss's birthday

TWO HOURS
of shredding
incriminating
documents

. . . Personal or professional documents

THREE
HOT
SALES
LEADS

*Valid for only recently deceased
or bankrupt clients*

Love in an Elevator: And Other Fun Ways to Pass the Time If You're Stuck in an Elevator

Unless you work on the first floor, you're going to spend at least a few socially awkward minutes each day in the elevator. You could just avoid eye contact like everybody else. Or you could make the most of your journey. Here are some tips to turn even the most tiresome elevator ride into a fun-filled (and occasionally bizarre) adventure:

Refuse to let anybody touch the floor buttons, insisting that you can control the elevator "with my mind."

↑

Make eye contact with your fellow passengers; deep, meaningful eye contact that seems to say, "I have found my soul mate."

↓

Take out a slip of paper and yell, "Come on! Come on, seven!" After you pass the seventh floor, yell in victory and hug your fellow passengers.

↑

Tap on a wall and offhandedly comment: "Boy, if you strangled someone in one of these, I bet nobody on the outside could even hear it."

Love in an Elevator

Take out a measuring tape and measure the floor. Write down the numbers and then say, "I'm a carpet installer, but I'm just starting out small to see if I like it."

⬆

When the doors open, look amazed. "What the hell? This doesn't look like the same place I got in. What demon's work is this?"

⬇

Press all the buttons. As the doors open at each floor, poke your head out, look around, and say, "Damn it. Where did I park my car?"

⬆

Make commentary on each and every floor in an exaggerated 1940s radio voice: "Third floor: lingerie, ladies' hats. Fourth floor: sporting goods." This is especially annoying in an eighty-floor office tower.

⬇

Tell everyone about the headline you saw in *USA Today:* "Modern Elevators Become Plummeting Boxes of Death." In retrospect, guess you should have read the article.

⬆

This Is Not a Drill

Even convicts get time in the yard. But *you*? You're chained to that desk forty-plus hours a week. That's why a fire drill out of the clear blue sky can be such a delicious, sinful experience. Make the most of your freedom with these helpful suggestions:

- Bring *all* of your belongings outside—including furniture, fax machines, and computer equipment. When the building has been cleared for reentry, request permission to permanently relocate your cubicle to the parking lot.
- Announce that "women and children" should be evacuated first, and then trample your coworkers in your rush for freedom. When questioned later, mumble something about having "the emotional maturity of a five-year-old child."
- Inform your superiors that an employee named "Johnson" is still missing. After a futile search, admit that Johnson is just your imaginary friend.
- Lead the entire crowd in a rousing chorus of "The roof, the roof, the roof is on fire." Continue long after it's become awkward.
- Transform a fire drill into an instant party by cooking a batch of homemade "third-degree-burn chili."
- Volunteer to be fire marshal, and proceed to run fire drills like a fascist regime. Demand complete submission from coworkers. If they resist your orders, scream, "Do you want to die?! Do you? *Do you?*"
- Ask the firefighters if you can sit in their truck. Because, c'mon, how cool is *that*?

You've Unleashed a Virus: Now What?

You accidentally download a file and discover too late that it might contain a virus. Or worse still, you inadvertently send the virus to your coworkers, spreading the infection to the entire company. What steps should you take to minimize the damage?

Cover Your Tracks

Take a few sick days and wait for the virus to be discovered by somebody else. When you finally return to the office, loudly say something like, "I go away for two lousy days and this happens?"

Bully the Tech Guy

Sure, your company's technical support guy may be able to fix the problem, but he may trace it to you. A couple of "noogies" should bring up enough painful childhood memories to keep him at bay for days.

Install Antivirus Software

Then say something like, "Well, I guess this is one of those new viruses that McAfee doesn't know about yet."

Give Your Virus a Catchy Name

If you're "patient 0," try endearing the virus to your coworkers by giving it a friendly and fun name like "ILOVEYOUKITTENPANTS" or "GIGABYTE GO BYE-BYE."

Chapter 9

Break Time

Top Ten Gags to Play on Coworkers

TOP 10

Sometimes a good-natured prank played on a co-worker can bring a little sunshine to the office. And if a good-natured prank can bring a *little* sunshine, these should deliver a supernova!

1. Change the caller ID on a coworker's phone to read "Mr. Kitten."
2. Steal random objects—such as staplers and phone headsets—from a coworker's desk and place them in the vending machine.
3. Using Photoshop, create a fake paycheck stub with your name on it and twice your normal salary amount; then leave it lying around the office. If someone remarks on your inflated salary, say, "Why? What are they paying you?"
4. Break into a coworker's car and fill it with live lobsters.
5. Hire someone to impersonate a police officer. Have him arrest a coworker during an important meeting with a new client.
6. Install a working urinal in a coworker's office.
7. Offer to do a tarot reading for your coworkers, providing only ambiguous predictions. "Well, that card either means great fortune or imminent death. I always forget."
8. Remove the shelves in the break room refrigerator and hide inside. Wait for somebody to open the door, and then jump out, screaming, "I am not a sandwich, damn you! I am a *human being!*"
9. Place a "Kick Me" sign on somebody's back. When your coworker fails to see the humor in your hack gag, slip into a deep depression. When he feels badly and tries to cheer you up, kick him squarely in the butt and scream, "Gotcha!"
10. Put a thousand loose marbles in the overhead cabinet in your office marked "Confidential."

Office Tattoos

The dress code don't say nothin' about ink! Well, unless you count paragraph four in section VI that forbids visible tattoos and soft tissue modification. In any case, even if they make you remove your tattoo you have to wait two weeks for the skin to heal. Here are some ideas for awesome office-themed tats.

"In Loving Memory of the Johnson Account—We Will Never Forget"

An illustration of Che Guevara holding a calculator triumphantly, accompanied by the words "La Revolución Accounting Department"

"O'Malley, Rubens, Conroy & Stiles Carpool Posse"

A weeping fairy sitting on a copier with an "Out of Order" sign on it

Full back piece of an Excel spreadsheet

Neck tattoo:
"Live fast, forced into early retirement with a pension that barely pays my mortgage young!"

Contest: Score Points for Office Dares

Not all office dares are created equal. It's one thing to convince a coworker to spend her entire business day skipping. It's quite another to coax her into doing it in a Boba Fett costume. For the newbie prankster, consult this helpful guide to the various levels of office dares—which includes a rudimentary scoring system.

Beginner Dares

When you enter the building in the morning, hold open the front door until someone approaches and then let it shut just before they get to it.

Use the intercom to page nonexistent employees, alternating between popular TV characters and deposed dictators.

Stare at a nonexistent spot on the ceiling until someone joins you.

Dare someone in Accounting to go the whole day without using the number four.

Call someone's $8^{1}/_{2}$-by-11 pad of paper an "illegal pad."

Stare at the vending machine until someone comes along and then say, "I don't think these big-screen HDTVs are so great."

Intermediate Dares

When a coworker is telling you an "interesting story" turn around and walk away in midsentence.

Call your boss "The Big Kahuna" for an entire day.

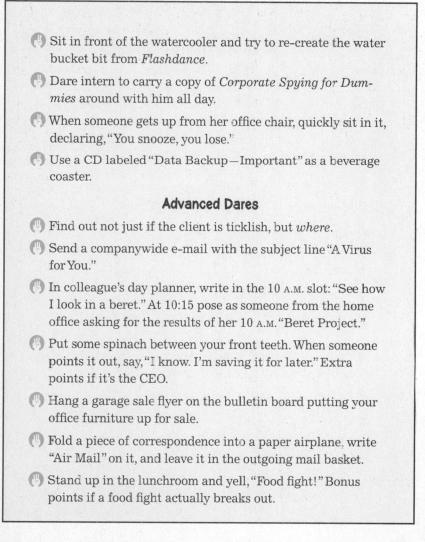

Sit in front of the watercooler and try to re-create the water bucket bit from *Flashdance*.

Dare intern to carry a copy of *Corporate Spying for Dummies* around with him all day.

When someone gets up from her office chair, quickly sit in it, declaring, "You snooze, you lose."

Use a CD labeled "Data Backup—Important" as a beverage coaster.

Advanced Dares

Find out not just if the client is ticklish, but *where*.

Send a companywide e-mail with the subject line "A Virus for You."

In colleague's day planner, write in the 10 A.M. slot: "See how I look in a beret." At 10:15 pose as someone from the home office asking for the results of her 10 A.M. "Beret Project."

Put some spinach between your front teeth. When someone points it out, say, "I know. I'm saving it for later." Extra points if it's the CEO.

Hang a garage sale flyer on the bulletin board putting your office furniture up for sale.

Fold a piece of correspondence into a paper airplane, write "Air Mail" on it, and leave it in the outgoing mail basket.

Stand up in the lunchroom and yell, "Food fight!" Bonus points if a food fight actually breaks out.

Simple Lunchtime Recipes

Every employee looks forward to lunch "hour"—the eight minutes you steal away to stuff something in your face while you catch up on work. But being stuck in the office doesn't mean you can't have a quality meal. Here are a few quick recipes for gourmet dishes you can prepare from the crap in the break room vending machines.

- ■ V-8 and Chiclets gazpacho

- ■ Beef jerky and Goldfish cracker surf and turf

- ■ Tic Tacs and nondairy creamer risotto

- ■ Popcorn flambé (Put bag of microwave popcorn in microwave. Cook on high for half an hour.)

- ■ Snicker sandwich on whole Twinkie bread

- ■ Peanut "gum"-bo (Mix dry-roasted peanuts and chewing gum.)

- ■ Country breakfast surprise (Microwave two hard-boiled eggs without piercing the shells—surprise!)

- ■ Slim Jims braised in room temperature cola

- ■ Oysters Newburg and cheese puffs (If your vending machine doesn't carry Oysters Newburg, substitute more cheese puffs.)

Time Killers: How to Look Busy Even When You're Not

Anybody can waste a business day playing online games or gazing at the clock. It takes a special talent to do nothing while creating the *illusion* that you're being productive. Here's a minute-by-minute guide to looking busy even when you're avoiding doing any actual work.

9:00–9:35 A.M.

Read all of your e-mails, even junk mail. Then print them out and read them again. Create a special file for your correspondence, organizing it by last name, date, category, and relevance.

9:36–9:57 A.M.

Test the ink supply of every pen on your desk. Don't be satisfied until you've filled at least twenty pages with little circles.

9:58–10:14 A.M.

Call coworkers in random order, asking, "Did you need to see me?" Continue until you've checked in with everybody in the building.

10:15–10:32 A.M.

Load your computer with unnecessary programs and wait for it to freeze. Then hit the Control-Alt-Delete buttons again and again and again and . . .

Time Killers: How to Look Busy Even When You're Not

10:33–11:29 A.M.

Sit in an empty conference room, doodling on a notepad and checking your watch. Eventually storm out and ask, "Why didn't anybody tell me that we'd canceled the morning meeting?"

11:30–11:59 A.M.

During a bathroom break, take your time washing your hands. Scrub every inch like doctors preparing for surgery. If confronted, insist that you're prone to staph infections.

NOON–1:45 P.M.

Agree to pick up lunch for the entire office. Drive to a restaurant that's several miles away, if possible in a different state.

1:46–2:06 P.M.

Dig through the wastebaskets in every room, claiming to have lost an important document. Continue your search outside in the company dumpsters.

2:07–2:28 P.M.

Somebody spilled coffee in the break room! Volunteer to clean up the mess, surrounding the area with police tape and carefully investigating the stain.

Time Killers: How to Look Busy Even When You're Not

2:29–3:07 P.M.

Make the rounds in the office, asking coworkers for updates on their projects. Just nod during their explanations and then say, "Well, it looks like you're on top of it."

3:08–3:41 P.M.

Wait until somebody is using the fax machine, then stand behind her and pretend to wait patiently for your turn. Repeat as necessary.

3:42–4:10 P.M.

Load and unload the copy machine, investigating a suspected paper clog. Try different colored paper, just to see if that fixes the problem. Give up in a fit of fury and make copies by hand instead.

4:11–4:53 P.M.

Sit in on a meeting that doesn't involve you. Listen quietly and pretend to take notes, occasionally saying something noncommittal like, "Good point."

4:54–5:00 P.M.

Start typing frantically, writing the same nonsense word repeatedly. Refuse to look up if a coworker interrupts you, saying only, "I gotta finish this report before the end of the day."

New Ideas for Breaks

Coffee breaks? Bathroom breaks? Smoke breaks? Amateur stuff. These are practically sanctioned by law. But if you play your cards right, you can add enough breaks into your workday so that the only thing interrupting your hours of creative goldbricking is . . . well . . . work. So, take a break.

> **SUDOKU BREAK.** No one will blame you for wanting to add a few numbers to the grid. And if you do it in a public area, your secretary, your manager—hell, even the CEO—will soon be looking over your shoulder trying to join in.

> **MOVIE BREAK.** Your boss expects you to stay connected to what's going on in the world so the company can profit from new trends, right? Well, what better way to do it than checking out the latest YouTube video? Maybe there are big bucks to be made investing in fat-guy-dancing-in-his-underwear futures.

> **EXERCISE BREAK.** The Japanese have known for years that lithe workers are productive workers. So what if your idea of exercise is bending over the doughnut box, craning your neck when that cute guy in Accounting goes by, or pushing away papers from

your in-box? Just accompany these moves by saying, "One-and-two-and . . . ," and suddenly they are exercise!

SPRING BREAK. See how many swigs of vodka you can take from your "water bottle" before coworkers start to notice your eyes glazing over and your speech slurring. Resist chanting, "Chug! Chug! Chug!" in response to "Where's the Malone report?" It's a dead giveaway.

COMPOUND FRACTURE BREAK. If you can stomach the pain, slamming your fingers into a drawer or inserting a pinkie in the paper shredder can get you a respite from your workday. Just show your boss the tiny bone protruding from your skin and he'll insist that you visit the emergency room.

PRISON BREAK. Build those valuable creativity skills that they're always harping about in productivity seminars. See if you can get out of the office and run some errands without anyone noticing you're gone.

Chapter 10

Happy Hour and Other Celebrations

Sobriety Test: Telltale Signs You've Had Too Much to Drink

There's nothing wrong with enjoying an after-work cocktail with your coworkers. But when "Happy Hour" turns into "Happy Early Morning," you may have taken the revelry just a little too far. How do you know when it's time to call it a night and stumble home? Here are some warning signs that you probably don't need to order another round:

- You've gone from drunk-dialing old boyfriends to drunk-dialing current clients.

- You've come up with some hilarious limericks about your boss, most of which involve him being from Nantucket.

- You start shouting "Free Bird" at the jukebox, apparently unaware that it is unlikely to respond.

- You have, in just fifteen minutes, proven the old maxim "Beer before liquor, never been sicker."

- You've spent the last hour talking to a coworker's identical twin, despite his insistence that he's an only child.

■ You've written the CEO's name in the bathroom stall, along with his personal cell phone number.

■ That's the third time somebody has told you, "Dude, that *isn't* a bathroom."

■ You're convinced the boss is hitting on you when he refers to "enhanced operational efficiencies."

■ Your karaoke rendition of "Baby Got Back" probably wasn't the best idea, especially as a slow, romantic serenade to the receptionist.

■ You could've sworn you came to the bar with pants.

■ You insist that you're sober enough to drive, despite the fact that you've been trying to start your car with a cocktail napkin.

■ You're wearing your tie on any part of your anatomy other than your neck.

Office Workers' Drinking Chart

Just about everyone enjoys a night out drinking with the co-workers. At some time in your career you will have to buy a coworker a drink...but what drink to buy for whom? Here's a handy chart for your reference:

Employee Type	Drink	Drink Description
The Safety Inspector	Three Mile Island Ice Tea	Like a Long Island Ice Tea, but with three times the liquor. Named so because it will make him have an "accident" in front of everyone that will take ages to clean up.
The Salesman Who Just Lost a Big Account	Absolutly Screwed	This lethal combination of Absolut vodka, triple sec, and OJ will dull the pain of screwing up until it is replaced by the pain of being fired.
Upper Management and VPs	The Hostile Takeover	Grain alcohol and red wine; this will knock them off the top floor and down to your level in no time!

Employee Type	Drink	Drink Description
Receptionist	Loose Lips	Vodka, coffee liqueur, and cola. Guaranteed to get her tipsy and keep her caffeinated long enough to spill the inside dirt she has on just about anyone!
The Out-of-Town Client Who's "On the Prowl"	Randy Alexander	This combination of brandy and crème de cacao will make them frisky, yet utterly resistible to the opposite sex.
Middle Management Stuffed Shirts	My Tie!	A powerful combination of rum and Wild Turkey that will have them puking on their tie before the night is over.
The Bean Counter	CPA	Citron, peach schnapps, and amaretto. This drink will make even the most boring number cruncher seem like Brad Pitt or Angelina Jolie by the bottom of the glass.
IT Guys	The Wrath of Quan	Four shots of Cointreau and a splash of Galliano. How do those programming skills help you now that you're drunk out in the real world, Nerd Boy?

Humorous Coasters: Put Them Under Your Glass and Let the Good Times Roll!

Most offices have a favorite watering hole where cube monkeys can meet to share a laugh and drown the reality of their bleak existence. Cut out one of these handy humorous coasters and slip it under a coworker's drink—you'll stave off the inevitable crying fit for hours!

This is my fourth— cancel the morning meeting!

I'm trying to kill enough brain cells to get promoted.

They can take away the health plan, but they can't keep me from self-medicating!

DESIGNATED DRIVER
(Put my scotch in a coffee mug.)

If you can read this, then buy me another drink.

I LOVE DRINKING WITH MY COWORKERS!

They're cooler than the tools at the office.

I'M IRISH.
What's your excuse?

Candy is dandy, but liquor is quickly destroying my liver.

I suck because work drinks!

Designated Drinker

I DON'T HAVE A DRINKING PROBLEM . . .

I drink, I get drunk, sometimes I don't remember how I got home, I missed my kid's . . . well whattaya know!

135

Icebreakers to Keep You and Your Coworkers from Talking About Work (for Thirty Seconds)

TOP 10

Nothing takes the fun out of socializing with your fellow employees like another redundant discussion about work. Don't let your next gathering devolve into pointless shoptalk. Here are ten icebreakers guaranteed to steer the conversation away from the office:

1. "This is some *crazy* weather we're having; it reminds me of my days back at the asylum."
2. "I love those shoes, did you make them yourself?"
3. "Am I the only one here who accidentally killed a hobo and then buried him in the desert? Come on, fess up. We're among friends."
4. "You know that hidden security camera they recently put in the employee lounge? Well, funny story . . ."
5. "You enjoy popular sporting events? What a coincidence! I enjoy popular sporting events!"
6. "I bet you can't guess my favorite Osmond!"
7. I read a great book over the weekend. What was it called? Oh, yeah, *People*.
8. I'm wearing underwear, but not where you'd think. Three guesses.
9. Let me tell you my favorite endings to the movies that came out last week . . .
10. Hey, my kid's home this weekend from Penn State. No, wait—the state pen. Why, what'd I say?

Holiday Party Mishaps

It's pah-tay time! Drinks, winks, and a whole lot of hijinks! If you find yourself putting the *s* in saucy, sharing secrets, or getting caught red-handed, remember there's a simple solution to every problem.

PROBLEM: Getting caught making out with your boss's spouse in the broom closet.
SOLUTION: "Good thing I knew CPR. But I absolutely refuse to take a reward!"

PROBLEM: Passing out from drinking way too much.
SOLUTION: Wear a medic alert bracelet identifying you as a diabetic narcoleptic.

PROBLEM: Spilling the beans on an interoffice romance.
SOLUTION: Cover it up by turning the whole holiday party into a giant game of "spin the bottle."

PROBLEM: Caught snooping in someone's office.
SOLUTION: Say you're on a candy cane hunt and the winner gets a new Toyota RAV4!

PROBLEM: You spill your drink on copier or other piece of expensive electronic equipment.
SOLUTION: Loudly boast, "Now they'll *have* to replace that old hunk of junk! This is my gift to all!"

PROBLEM: You forget to bring a gift for the Secret Santa exchange.
SOLUTION: Claim that your gift was "too large" to bring to the Christmas party. When asked about it later, mutter something about your gift being confiscated by the feds, as it was "apparently on some endangered species list."

How to Keep Your Job After Getting Saucy and Telling Off Your Boss

When you've had a bit too much to drink at an office party, it might be impossible not to tell your boss what you *really* think about him. If you make this unfortunate social faux pas with the Big Man, you're going to need a way to dig yourself out—fast. The next time you've put your foot in your mouth, consider the following strategies.

- Claim you have a recessive Tourette's gene that was only recently discovered. Quickly call your boss a "big, fat, loser, stupid son of a . . . ," then say, "See?"
- Avoid your boss for the rest of your career.
- Explain that in some societies "jackoff" is considered a term of great respect.
- Suggest that you have a slight speech impediment. You didn't call him a "prick"; you called him a "brick," the cornerstone of our proud firm.
- Tell him you're a mole for upper management and you were actually testing him on his ability to deal with hostile employees. Then congratulate him and present him with a certificate you made in Word.
- Go to your boss first thing in the morning and complain about what a lame "insult-and-obscenity-hurling party" that was last night. Ask who they insulted.
- Tell him you bet Myers in HR a *thousand* bucks that you wouldn't get fired after insulting the boss. Hand your boss five hundred bucks and tell him it's his cut for playing along.
- Sheepishly explain that you've always had a hard time expressing love.

The Anniversary Gift Catalog

Once you have truly settled into your office job, the years will start flying by quicker than a cat on meth. But don't let the rapidly increasing number of years you've spent thanklessly chained to you desk get you down. For every milestone year you stay on the job you get a swell anniversary gift!

1 YEAR
First anniversary is "paper."
Be thankful it's a crappy
certificate from the copy shop
rather than a pink slip.

5 YEARS
Department head begins
to remember your name.

10 YEARS
Li'l Decade, the Teeny Beanie
that cries when you squeeze it.

15 YEARS
A "gold" pin that leaves a
green ring on the lapels of
all your jackets.

20 YEARS
Company picks up the tip at a
luncheon held in your honor
(up to the customary eight percent).

25 YEARS
A commemorative watch
to remind you of the quarter
century of your life that you'll
never get back.

30 YEARS
You finally qualify for
health insurance.

35 YEARS
An all-expense-paid trip to
the North Dakota resort
of your choice.

40 YEARS
The ol' pink slip, six months before your pension is fully vested.

Chapter 11

I'm Outta Here!

Signs That You Should Run—
Not Walk—from Your Job!

In a perfect world, you'd want to stay at your company for the long haul, settling in until your eventual retirement. But sometimes you get a nagging feeling that you should get out before it's too late. And it's not always because of the usual complaints, like low salaries or inadequate opportunities for career advancement. Here are just a few indicators that you should consider cleaning out your desk *tout de suite*.

- Your company's new motto? "Hugs, not drugs."
- During off-site meetings, you're encouraged to "steal as much as you can grab."
- Your holiday bonus came from the annual canned food drive.
- Casual Fridays have been replaced with Litigious-Document Shredding Fridays.
- Four words: guys in hazmat suits.
- The company's hold music is Mozart's *Requiem*.
- The Christmas party is being sponsored by the Betty Ford Clinic.
- The CEO keeps insisting that you "try the poison pun—er, I mean the refreshing, nonpoisonous, nothing-to-do-with-a-cult-mass-suicide punch."
- Your cubicle is now equipped with bulletproof glass.
- You're the only member of senior management not currently serving prison time.
- On at least one occasion, you've walked in on your boss having a conference call with the United Nations, in which you could've sworn he said, "And then I will destroy you all! Bwah-ha-ha-ha!"
- Michael Moore has been hanging out in the lobby more than usual.

Start Your Own Business Kit

When your company announces cutbacks on your benefits because the CEO got caught "investing" at an offshore casino, you might think it's time to get off the corporate merry-go-round. "This is it," you tell yourself. "I'm quitting this hellhole and starting my own business. I couldn't run it half as bad as this group of numb nuts. I'll show them. I'll show them all!" (Just make sure you don't tell yourself all this out loud.) Here's everything you'll need to break out on your own.

BUSINESS CARDS.
Nontraditional business cards that stand out from the crowd are all the rage nowadays. Consider hand-printing your contact information on a piece of bologna, with the slogan "No Baloney. Jim Larson is the best!"

TITLE.
Choose something like "Business Consultant" or "Corporate Coach." This will allow you to charge top dollar without ever having to explain what you do or produce measurable results.

DIPLOMAS.
No one ever checks someone's college records, so go nuts! Some parchment paper from the office supply store and the Old English font in your word processor—and you have credentials from Harvard, Yale, and Oxford without having to pay those hefty tuitions.

Start Your Own Business Kit

COMPANY NAME.
Nothing says "I have my own business" like a catchy name for your company. Pick a name that's instantly memorable and maybe a little bizarre. When in doubt, just combine a random color with an animal: for example, Blue Fox, Red Hawk, Violet Wombat. Oh yeah. They smell like money.

LOGO.
Without a trademark symbol to adorn your new company's stationery, nobody will ever take you seriously. You could pay a lot of money to a graphic designer. Or just do what everyone else does and put a capital letter in a weird font inside a circle or a square.

OFFICE SUPPLIES.
Plan ahead and start taking home a few supplies from your current employer. Grab as many pens, pads, and copier toner as you can steal. Anything that isn't nailed down is fair game. And if you manage to hide the copy machine under your coat without being noticed, it's yours for the taking.

SOFTWARE.
It is a crime to pirate software. So never do it at sea, but only on dry land.

TOP 10

Surefire Ways to Get Fired

So, you're ready to quit your job, but quitting is just one more action item in your in-box. Why should you do all the work? Use one (or more) of these techniques and make the HR rep fire you (you'll collect unemployment that way!).

1. Tattoo biggest competitor's logo on forehead.
2. Repeatedly call in sick with "the farts."
3. Loudly boast to your higher-ups that you traded valuable company secrets for "magic beans."
4. Proclaim your cubicle as the independent nation of No-pants-istan and declare war on the United States.
5. Buy yourself a $60,000 sports car; have vanity plates read "MBEZ-ZLR."
6. Start bringing in live poultry to kill in the break room for lunch.
7. Slowly start dressing more and more like a clown over a few weeks.
8. End every PowerPoint presentation with that picture of you passed out in Cancún.
9. Sell equipment from the office on eBay.
10. Start leaving the office at 3:30 every day, loudly declaring, "Beer-thirty! Quitting time!"

Mad Lib Résumé

Most résumés are interchangeable anyway, so don't waste hours creating a new one when your potential employer is only going to spend seven seconds reading it. Just fill in the blanks below.

CAREER OBJECTIVE

Seeking a position with a major

heading from yellow pages

where my experience as a

name of job two levels above any position you've ever held

can be utilized to help   achieve

name of company you're applying to

title of a speech from Mussolini

QUALIFICATION SUMMARY

-               of experience in the

Your age minus ten years   noun chosen from recent cover of

industry.

Forbes

Mad Lib Résumé

- Created _____ Department, increasing sales
  <small>synonym for business</small>

  by _____ percent.
  <small>two rolls of D&D dice</small>

- Initiated study to ensure compliance with

  _____ , _____ Act.
  <small>name of a senator</small>   <small>name of another senator</small>

- Introduced _____ Report, which _____
  <small>Greek letter</small>   <small>any verb ending in "ized"</small>

  information.

- Won _____ award three years running.
  <small>Waspy Anglo-Saxon name</small>

PROFESSIONAL EXPERIENCE

_____ **TO THE PRESENT**
<small>Year you graduated college</small>

- Professional _____
  <small>title of a job that sounds way cooler than your actual last job</small>

147

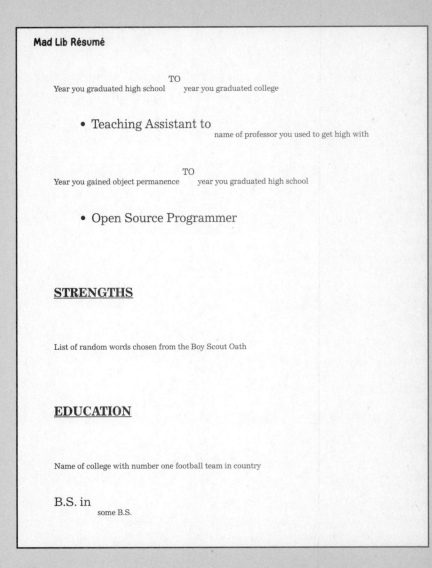

Mad Lib Résumé

TO
Year you graduated high school   year you graduated college

- Teaching Assistant to
  name of professor you used to get high with

TO
Year you gained object permanence   year you graduated high school

- Open Source Programmer

STRENGTHS

List of random words chosen from the Boy Scout Oath

EDUCATION

Name of college with number one football team in country

B.S. in
  some B.S.

Training Courses You Should Take Before Your New Job

Braving a new office world can be scary. Make sure to sign up for these must-have courses so you're prepared to take on all the new crazies at your next job and maybe even become their leader.

Dealing with Difficult People: *How to Make It Look Like an Accident*

Technical Writing: *Not* Technically *Writing*

Grammar for Businesspeople: English as a First Language

Personality Testing: *Boiling Down Years of Life Experience to Two Letters and a Color*

Interviewing Skills: *How to Tell the Idiots from the Lazy*

Getting Things Done . . . So Your Boss Can Give You Even More Things to Do

Persuasive Writing . . . Oh, Never Mind . . .

Managing Chaos (Otherwise Known as Your Job)

Project Management Skills: *Finding the Perfect Scapegoat*

Management Skills for Advancement: *How to Suck Up Without Being Labeled a Suckup*

Effective Meetings: *An Oxymoron*

Public Speaking, Private Weeping

Retaining Customers for Life (Until They Find a Lower Price Through One of Your Competitors)

Leadership Skills: *Shut Up and Get Out of the Way*

Delegating Effectively: *"Not It!"*

Six Sigma Quality: *It's All Greek to Me*

Assertiveness Training—Unless You Don't Think You Can Handle It, Loser

Communication and Interpersonal Skills: *Faking Sincerity*

The Secret to Making Big Money in the Seminar Business: *Only $495*

Resignation Text Messages

Proper etiquette dictates that you should write a letter of resignation before leaving a job. But this is the twenty-first century! Why write a letter when sending a simple text message will do? Below is a list of sample text templates you can use the next time you give notice.

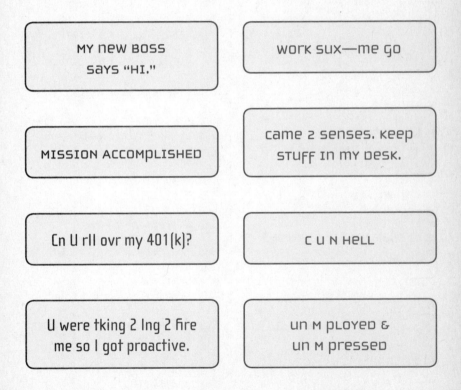

> MY new BOSS SaYS "HI."

> work SUX—me go

> MISSION ACCOMPLISHED

> came 2 senses. keep STUFF in mY DeSK.

> Cn U rll ovr my 401(k)?

> C U N HeLL

> U were tking 2 lng 2 fire me so I got proactive.

> un M pLOYeD & un M preSSeD

I'M FIRED! (YOU'LL FIND OUT WHY BY END OF THIS quarter.)

It's over (sent from saved text you sent fiancé).

I QUIT—can I STILL use copier?

Working from home today (but not 4 U!)

U were crappy boss. Hope U make better reference!

LOST MY OFFICE ID— ceased 2 EXIST

Last report I sent was all lies—L8TR!

Sent copy of *Cube Monkeys: A Handbook for Surviving the Office jungle* to all Fortune 500 companies. Bound to get great job offer soon!

Chillin@home. Send severance package.

About the Authors

ED FURMAN has cowritten numerous theatrical pieces including Chicago's longest-running musical, *Co-ed Prison Sluts*. He has written jokes for a wide variety of folks including Martin Short, Scooby-Doo, and the Chicago History Museum.

KIRK HANLEY started his career as an automotive engineer before quitting and making the natural transition to acting and comedy writing. Oddly enough, both industries benefited from this change. He has cowritten many plays and revues, including (with Maribeth Monroe) the national tours of *My Cousin's Wedding* and *Sex and the Second City*.

ERIC SPITZNAGEL is a frequent contributor to magazines like *Playboy, Esquire, The Believer*, and Salon.com, among many others. He's the author of six books, including *A Junk Food Companion* (Dutton, 1999) and *A Guy's Guide to Dating* (Doubleday, 1998).

CONTRIBUTING WRITERS from CareerBuilder.com: Jennifer Sullivan, Kate Lorenz, and Michael Erwin